PAPER SCULPTURE

Revised and Enlarged

MARY GRACE JOHNSTON
Supervisor of Art Education
Newark, New Jersey
Public Schools

DAVIS PUBLICATIONS, INC. - WORCESTER, MASSACHUSETTS

The author gratefully acknowledges the generous help
of those who have contributed their time, their
experience and their understanding:

Dr. Edward F. Kennelly, *Superintendent of Schools, Newark, New Jersey*

Ralph M. Lordi, *Director, Art Education Department, Newark Public Schools*

William Harrison Horney, *Photographer, Newark, New Jersey*

Walter E. Haggerty, *J. L. Hammett Company, Union, New Jersey*

Paul Goward, *Shrewsbury, Massachusetts*

Al Opie, *O-P Craft Company, Sandusky, Ohio*

Bertram Cholet, *Higgins Ink Co., Brooklyn, New York*

Hunt Manufacturing Company, *Camden, New Jersey*

Minnesota Mining and Manufacturing Company, *St. Paul, Minnesota*

Prang Studio, *The American Crayon Company, New York City*

Contents

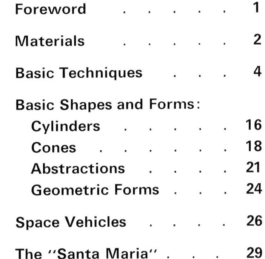

To
Dorothy Curtis Johnston
and
Francis Carroll Johnston

FOREWORD

This revision of "Paper Sculpture" (1952) and "Paper Shapes and Sculpture for School Use" (1956), combined under one cover, has attempted to retain and include only those pages and materials that have already established teacher value and pupil worth through classroom use over a period of years. In addition, many new photographs of advanced paper sculpture, significant for school use have been included.

Paper sculpture affords a unique challenge to the creativity and imagination of the artist. It enjoys proved and limitless value as an avenue of self-expression and can be readily and easily utilized in teaching the basic principles of space, organization and design. Every normal child possesses a marked and meaningful degree of creativity, even though obviously not all children are endowed with unlimited creative potential. It is hoped that the photographs, designs, and delineations in this book will help children in classrooms across the nation to explore their replete reservoirs of ideas and to experience that intimate delight that results only from the opportunity to produce tangible evidence and artistic reflection of their personal vision. It should also assist them to channel their activities into deeper and more extensive art experiences.

It should be noted here that the author of the current revision of her 1952 and 1956 publications in the area of paper sculpture, as a meaningful vehicle in the boundless field of art education, is eminently fitted by professional preparation, practical teaching and supervisory experience and professional skill and dedication, to bring it to the teachers and pupils of America. She is indeed sharing the dividends of a lengthy and pertinent professional career in art in public education.

I am indebted professionally to Miss Mary Grace Johnston for the many years of valuable instructional and supervisory service she has given to the Newark Public Schools. I am indebted personally to her for the privileged invitation to contribute this foreword to a publication that is destined to be educationally valuable to thousands of boys and girls in order that their art education experiences may be more meaningful, creative and personal.

EDWARD F. KENNELLY
Superintendent of Schools
Newark, New Jersey

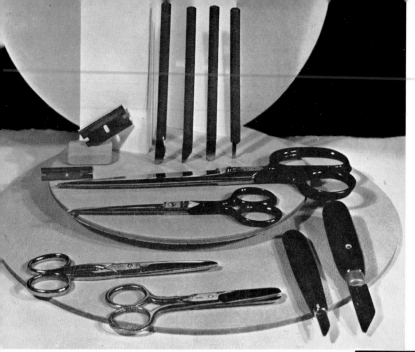

TO CUT

1. Scissors with blunted points
2. Regulation schoolroom scissors
3. Banker's shears
4. Frisket type knives
5. Dexter knives
6. Industrial one-edged razor blade
7. Heavy cardboard mats

TO SCORE

1. Scissor blade
2. Frisket type knife
3. Wooden modeling tool
4. Steel knitting needle
5. Steel rule
6. Metal-edged ruler
7. Plastic draftsman's angle
8. Compass

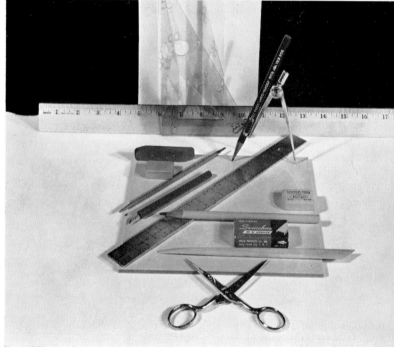

TO FASTEN

1. Transparent scotch tape
2. Masking tape, single and double faced
3. Scotch tape dispenser
4. Higgins vegetable glue
5. Small stapler
6. Large eye needle and thread
7. Stapler
8. Sobo, a white plastic glue.

MATERIALS

The artist who models in paper is striving for the same quality in his work as the sculptor who models in clay or chips away at stone until his design emerges. Paper sculpture is the art of forming figures or designs in relief, in intaglio, or in the round by cutting, scoring, bending and manipulating paper. This medium may lack some of the stability of clay, stone and wood, but for what it lacks in that direction, it more than makes up in flexibility and adaptability.

The first requirement for success in paper sculpture is the right kind of paper. It must be of a quality that is strong, firm and tractable; it must be depended on to fold without breaking, curl without shredding and hold in place when it is fixed. The paper used must be able to withstand considerable handling and stay crisp and fresh. Paper that has a tendency to dry out and become brittle should be avoided. The beginning paper sculptor needs all the confidence and encouragement he will gain from working with fine paper.

It is wise to limit the size of the sheet of paper in classroom work. Pieces too large to be easily accommodated on a table top or classroom desk have been found to be impractical, awkward and unwieldy. Packaged sheet paper can be handled and stored better than paper in a roll. If a large curved surface is needed, roll one sheet at a time, tightly or loosely, according to the curve desired, and leave it in this position for a time. It will absorb enough moisture from the air to keep it curved.

Youngsters, experimenting with paper as a medium of design, need room in which to work. They also need an adequate flat surface on which to spread out their materials and tools. Table tops and desks should be protected with a sheet of gray chip board, which when cut into or pressed on has just the right amount of "give."

Let every "smidgen" of each sheet of paper be used, saving all odd shapes and cutaway pieces for future use. Some of the most interesting and original free flowing designs result from using bits of what would otherwise be waste paper.

It is a good plan to provide each young artist with a large paper shopping bag into which he may discard too small pieces of waste. It is so much easier to "pick up" as one goes along than to clean up at the end of the day.

White paper was used to design all the illustrations in this book for two reasons: first, the camera picks up every gradation from light to dark, and second, the end result has a more sculptured effect. For the younger student, however, colored papers provide an extra appeal and may be more practical, since they do not have to be kept as clean and untouched in appearance as the white.

The photographed illustrations on the following pages were done in either "Hammett's 00 Heavy White Drawing Paper, or Strathmore Alexis White Water Color Paper." The drawing paper is excellent for all designs displayed on panels measuring 22 x 30 inches or for figures up to 24 inches in height, while the heavier, tougher water-color paper will support itself on a much larger scale.

The following papers are recommended for use in schools for young people.
1. Hammett's 00 Heavy White Drawing Paper, 9 x 12, 12 x 18, 18 x 24 inches.
2. Hammett's Colored Construction Paper in White, Black, Gray, Flesh and 24 colors—100 sheets per package, 18 x 24 inches.
3. Hammett's Art Mounts in bright colors and white and gold, 20 x 26 inches.
4. Strathmore Alexis Water Color Paper, 22 x 30 inches.
5. Hawthorne Folding Bristol (colored tag), 18 x 24 inches.
6. Hammett's Forbon in black and white.

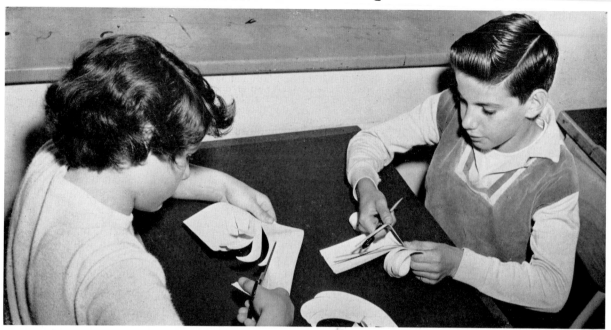

Cutting with Scissors

The quality of line produced by a cut edge plays an important part in paper sculpture design. This edge must be clean, free-flowing and continuous. Young children should use blunt pointed, but sharp bladed scissors, until they have gained some experience. Then they will find that the longer and sharper the scissor blades are, the smoother and more certain the cut edge will be.

The paper should be firmly held in one hand and moved into the jaws of the closing blades of the scissors worked with the other hand. Never chop into paper with the scissors. In the hands of an experienced person a sharp pair of scissors will slice through paper without closing and opening the blades.

Short, sharp knife blades are necessary to cut slits and slashes within the shape and the frisket type knife with the long handle and short blade is handy and safe for children. A knife is also needed to cut a true straight edge against a metal-edged ruler. When a knife or razor blade is used, the paper should lie flat on the table or desk, and care should be taken that the hand with the knife is directed away from the hand holding the paper. Best results are obtained by starting the cut away from the hand and towards the person who is cutting. In paper sculpture design the clean sweep of a cut line can be most attractive.

Scoring and Folding

Scoring paper consists of pressing a fine, deep, incisive line into paper, so that with slight pressure the paper will bend along the line and fall away on different planes. Scoring first on one side and then the other produces shadows that suggest depth in the pattern.

In the beginning, a student tends to press too hard on his tool, cutting through instead of making an engraved line. A little practice will give him a feeling for the right amount of pressure. The safest method of scoring is to use the rounded back edge of a scissors blade, the tip of a steel knitting needle or crochet hook, or the rounded point of a wooden modeling tool, pressed into the paper with a deliberate but free flowing and direct motion. The tip of a dull knife or the point of a used commercial razor blade must be used with delicacy and precision.

Scoring paper makes it possible to show deep and shallow folds, pleats and wrinkles in clothing, veins and structural lines in flowers and leaves. Scoring and folding paper is the full substance of paper sculpture.

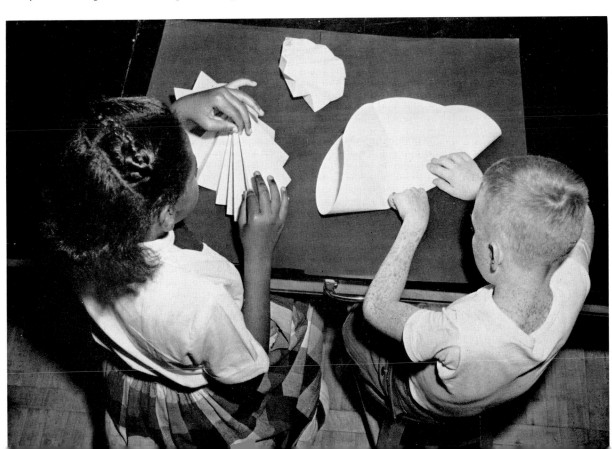

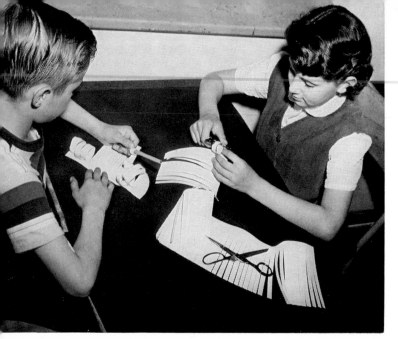

Curling Paper with Blade

Hold the strip of paper to be curled in one hand. With the other hand, take hold of the piece to be curled between the thumb and the edge of the scissors blade. Draw the scissors edge against the paper from start to finish of the strip, always pressing the paper firmly to the blade. This will result in anything from a slight curve to a real curl, all depending on the amount of pressure applied when sliding the paper between the thumb and the blade. If a very tight curl is desired, wind the paper back into a spiral position, holding it in place for a few moments before allowing it to loosen.

In curling a ribbon end, or a waving pennant, press and pull against the scissors, first on one side and then on the opposite side. The curved directions may be rearranged with the fingers.

When planning to use many separate curls, cut the strips in a fringe. After curling they may be cut apart singly or in sections.

Curling Paper with Pencil

If the problem is something like a wig or a woolly lamb, it will be necessary to curl many strips of paper. A quick method is to take three strips at a time, wind them over and over on the pencil, moisten slightly and allow to dry. This can be done at least six times on one pencil or other slender cylindrical stick. Wrap the pencil in a single sheet of paper until the curls are dry so that they will stay in position and not unwind. Slip the rings of paper off the pencil, separate the curls and pull them out to the desired length.

Ringlets can be made by wrapping long strips of paper around the pencil, continuously. The strips must be caught at either end with scotch tape so that they will not unwind until ready.

To curl a curved strip, place the pencil on the tip of the piece of paper and curl the paper up the side of the pencil and recurl with the fingers.

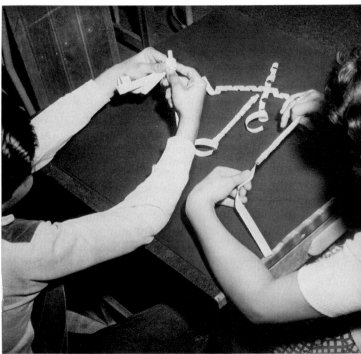

Pressing Paper into Place

Patience, a delicate handling of the material, and persistence contribute to the final beauty and success of paper sculpture. First, cut the basic shapes, next score the pattern of ridges and depressions, then with skill and sensitivity, press, bend and twist the paper until it falls into the proper position. Never force the direction. Ease and coax the the paper to take the position required of it.

Success in manipulating paper depends on remembering that scored lines must be parallel, or ray out from a single point and take the same direction, whether on a straight line or a curved line. Never try curves in opposition to each other. When scored lines crisscross each other on opposite sides of the paper, it helps in pressing these lines into position if a small opening is cut inside the crossed lines.

Much of the pleasure in creative paper design comes from being able to make the material do the bidding of the artist. "If at once you don't succeed, try, try again."

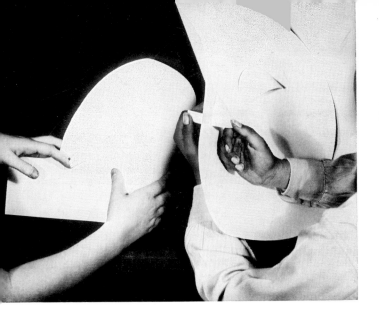

Fasten with Scotch Tape

For the many times when the child wants to fasten one paper shape to another without showing the connection, Scotch Brand Pressure-Sensitive Tape is absolutely indispensable.

Slits should be cut in the paper which is used as the background piece, and projecting tabs can be left along the edge of the paper which is to be fastened to the background. When the tabs are inserted into the slits, the applied piece of paper curves out and in again and appears to be of one piece with the background. To fasten the thrust-through tabs securely to the back of the design, a short length of pressure-sensitive tape should be pressed over the loose tab and the surrounding area. The tape must lie flat over the joined pieces, and all edges and corners must be pressed firmly and evenly into the paper. For all points of fastening not directly exposed to the viewer of the design, Scotch Brand Pressure-Sensitive Tape is the ideal adhesive.

Build from a Base

Paper sculptured figures, animals, and abstractions modeled "in the round" should be supported and given stability by a center shaft, which can be a slender cylinder or a pyramid, fastened obliquely or at right angles with pressure-sensitive tape to a heavy cardboard base.

Such bases can be obtained from the O-P Craft Company, of Sandusky, Ohio, which manufactures and distributes a heavy cardboard plaque, in various geometric shapes and various sizes. The plaques are of an agreeable light cream color, accurately die cut, and thick and sturdy though light in weight. They make ideal bases and can be used over and over again. They may also be used for tracing exact squares or triangles before the child knows how to use the compass and the T-square.

To fasten a cylindrical shaft to a base, cut one end of the cylinder into strips that can be spread apart and folded outward to lie flat on the base. The strips can then be fastened to the base with small pieces of pressure-sensitive tape.

In the use of such small amounts of Scotch Brand Tape, the dispenser shown in the photograph at the right eliminates waste by making the exact amount needed available at any time.

The three- or four-sided pyramid is easier to build than the cylinder, but it can be used only as part of the design, as in an abstraction requiring a pyramidal supporting piece, or as a support for a skirted figure.

Tack and Join

There is seldom a need for a wide variety of glues, cements, tapes, and tack together tools, but the young artist in paper sculpture will do work far in advance of his years if he has on his work table, one good glue, an adhesive tape, and either a needle and thread or a small stapler.

Higgins Vegetable Glue is excellent for paper sculpture. It is most efficient when a small amount is used, and may be applied with a paste brush or with a finger tip. It will hold paper together fast and forever. The glue stays moist a long time when exposed to the air.

Besides the variety of tape mentioned above, there is also "Scotch Brand Pressure-Sensitive Tape, No. 400," which is sticky on both sides and has an extremely strong grip. A small piece applied to one section of paper sculpture and pressed hard against another is sufficent for a firm and complete fastening. The tape must be kept separated, as it is being cut, from its non-sticky protecting strip. If too much tape is cut off at one time, it will be hard to handle, since it is very sticky. As in the illustration on the left, it is advisable to let one child cut and dole out each piece to the child who is using it for fastening.

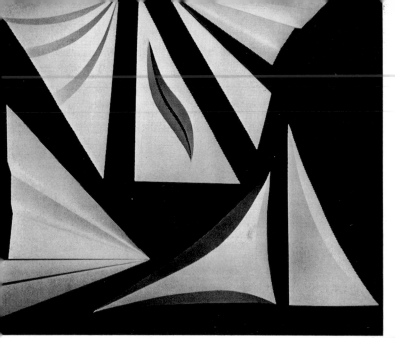

Folds in Triangular Shapes

Shadowed surfaces are an important part of paper modeling and paper sculpture. This appearance of depth comes about when paper is scored and folded. In the illustrations on this page are several ways of getting certain results; straight, curved and reverse curved folds. The same steps would be taken if the basic shape was square, rectangular or irregular.

In the first triangular shape in the upper left-hand corner of the illustration, left, the folds are curved in one direction. Score from a single point, in this case a corner, swing the first line in an easy, continuous motion, and let all other lines follow, allowing the distance between the lines to widen as they go. Turn the paper over and score the same number of lines from the same point. The amount of space left between the lines will determine the depth of the fold. Press the scored lines on opposite sides of the paper into place.

The upper center shape, at left, has been slashed in a slightly reversed curve cut. On the same side of the paper on each side of the cut, a line has been scored from end

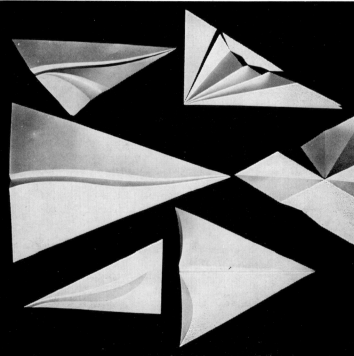

to end of cut and pressed back. It is the double curve opening that makes possible the effect of a hollow shape.

The last piece of paper on the top line has been scored and folded in a knife pleat, all lines starting from a single point, broadening toward the end.

In the lower row, above, the left-hand example shows a flat center section like a box pleat with flat pleats or folds continuing on either side. To have a fold lie almost flat score the underneath line a short distance away from the line on the top side. Again score and fold all lines from a single point. This all makes for a finer finish to the complete design.

The last two shapes, above, have been scored and folded back in a curved direction from corner to corner, only on one side of the paper. This is a way to show a spear or arrowhead. One side curved in gives a triangular shape a billowing look.

In the upper right-hand corner of the photograph to the right, two identical shapes are shown. One is flat and the other has been folded into a winglike form.

At the right a triangular shape with equal sides has been scored and folded from a center point in even sections. Measuring here is unnecessary if the even triangle is folded corner to corner. After all the folds are made in one direction reverse every other one and press into place. The

other shapes shown here have been scored, once in the center, on one side, and twice on the opposite side, on either side of the first fold. This fold will be used often for stems, veins in leaves and other center divisions.

Folds in opposition to each other are possible only when an absolute center is used and the scoring and folding starts equidistant from the center line. As in the left-hand triangle in the photograph to the left, score and fold increasingly curved lines from the point away from the center.

In the three-cornered shape at the bottom, a point within the triangle has been established by scoring and folding a curved line from first corner to second corner. Starting at some point on this line, score and fold back on a line to the third corner. Turn the paper over and proceed from the same center point to score and fold a line on both sides of each fold. This type of fold is possible in any shape.

The top example shows what happens when a curved line from corner to corner is scored and folded on either side of the paper.

There is a freshness and spontaneity to a paper sculptured line that is not easy for children to achieve in other media.

Folds in Circular Shapes

Circular shapes can be given a variety of sculptured forms and will show the young artist how accurate planning and skillful handling are essential for good results.

Having found the center point with a compass or by folding the paper twice at right angles, the student can use the radius of the circle to divide the circumference into six parts. Then he can fold the paper into six sections and fold each section in half again around the outer edge to get twelve even divisions.

Always fold a circular shape from edge to edge *through the center point,* if the folds are to be in a straight line. If the folds radiate from a center and you wish the form to lie flat, cut a circular opening and press the folded edges toward this center hole. There are several ways of turning the opening into a decorative detail in the design.

In the illustration at right, the circular shape at the top has been folded six times through the center with every other fold to the center reversed.

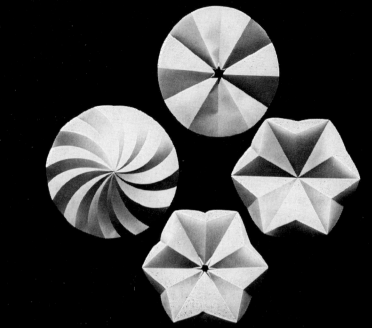

At right, in the illustration above, the center of the circular shape remains unaltered, but symmetrical lines have been scored within each sector from a point in the circumference where the radius meets the edge to a point at equal distances from each of these intersection points. At these points break the fold so that the line is reversed to form a star-shaped pattern. The third design (bottom) is similar except it has an opening in the center in the form of a six-pointed star.

The unit at the left in this group, showing a swirl pattern within a circular shape, has been divided into even parts with a compass. Place the point of the compass on the edge of the circular piece of paper, and with a radius equal to the radius of the circle involved, draw a curved line from the center point to the outside edge. Move the point around the circular edge, and at regular measured intervals, draw with the same radius, lines connecting the center point to the outside edge. These curved lines will reverse their direction from circumference edge, through the center point, and on to the opposite edge. Score and fold the entire curved line, one at a time, clear around the circle, all on the one side of the paper. After these curved lines have been sharply creased, reverse every other fold and press into place.

In the photograph at left, upper left and upper right, are two rosette forms developed with concentric circles. For these circular patterns a compass is a "must." Let the compass point make a clear mark through to the other side of the paper, for it is used for circles on

both sides. Now, make as many circles within this shape as you wish, first on one side, then on the other. Score each curved line carefully, keeping to the penciled line. Before trying to fold the scored lines, cut from the edge to the center in a straight or slightly curved line.

In the lower right-hand corner of this cluster of patterns above is a circular shape with lines and folds radiating from a point off center in a shell-like design. If the edge is scalloped, it looks even more like a shell, and there are still other ways of treating the edge.

On an outside curve of paper it is always possible to send a part in toward the center but never out away from the surface curve. In the photograph at right, in the upper left-hand corner is a section of a cone, with semi-circular areas depressed on either side of the upper edge. A bent-in curve like this will accommodate another curved shape, such as a cone or a cylinder, so that one form appears to be a part of the other, and of one piece.

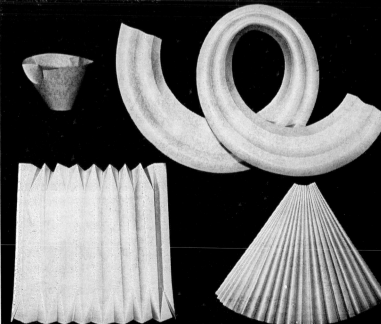

Shadow Folds

AS DARK AND LIGHT play an important part in paper sculpture, so do the folds that are responsible for the contrasts. Bend a sheet of paper along a straight line and note that one side catches the light, leaving the other side in shadow. If the paper is folded into several parallel creases, turned over, and folds made between the first creases, the result will be a series of reverse folds. These break up a flat surface into a pattern of light and dark.

On the opposite page, and in the diagram below, are a few of the folds used in designing paper-sculptured compositions. Any fold which suggests the third dimension is acceptable.

One of the most satisfying designs and certainly one of the simplest, is the rosette of concentric circles. Use a round shape a third again as large as you want it to be when finished. Divide with a compass into concentric circles, using the same center, and repeat on the opposite side. Score circles one, three and five on one side, and two, four and six on the other side, using a dull razor blade. Cut out a small wedge shape at an angle of about twenty degrees from circumference to center. Press gently along each scored curved line until you have a sharp edge. Do this first on one side, then on the other. When all the folds are sharp and crisp, fasten the two cut edges together, deepening the depth of the folds in the process. Arrange the circles as unevenly as you wish for variety in design.

To get the effect of wavy or chevronlike stripes, it is best to first lay out the surface of the sheet into a trellis of regular squares or rectangles. These divisions are shown in the two center units in the diagrams. Score the diagonals in a continuous line alternately on one side, then on the reverse side. Press each line to a sharp crease. In all the diagrams a solid line indicates an edge or a line scored on the right side. A dotted line means a scored line on the back of the paper. Coax the folds into position, keeping in mind that at each break or change in direction, the fold is reversed. The curved or wavy fold is made by scoring a regular reversed curved line and repeating a parallel curved line, scoring on alternate sides of the paper.

The triangle illustrated is divided into folds which are straight at one edge but curve more each time a fold is made—a gradual change from a straight fold to a curved fold. The section or segment of the circle shown is pressed into rippled curves which are narrow at the top growing wider toward the bottom edge.

The five-pointed star is a popular spot shape. It may be cut from a folded sheet of paper with a single stroke. Fold a thin piece of paper in half. From the center of the crease, fold over enough to equal one-fifth of a straight angle. Turn back the larger angle so that the original center fold lies along the first fold. Now you should have what appears to be two equal angles. Fold back a third time and cut at a sharp angle. The five-pointed shape must be refolded so that the center of each point is an up fold and the other a reverse fold. If the star shape is to be made of heavy paper, it is wiser to cut a pattern in thin stock and trace around the edge onto heavier material.

Through experiments in cutting and folding, many novel results are possible. Those that are illustrated represent only a very few.

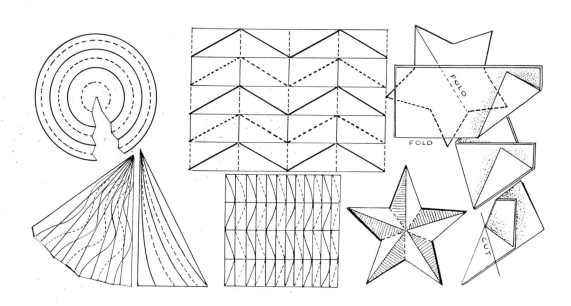

10

Cut Surface Designs and Abstract Shapes

CUTTING into the paper at regular intervals, a slanted or curved opening transforms a flat sheet into a design of light and shadow. These designs make interesting backgrounds in themselves or break up a surface within a large mass. This method of creating contrasts is good for suggesting feathers on birds and petals on flowers. Illustrated on the opposite page and in the diagram below are some combinations of cutting strokes that produce a wide variety of designs. If the design is to cover a large area, lay out a background of geometric divisions in light pencil strokes. Any of the arrangements commonly used to repeat a design such as the checkerboard, the half over or half drop, the diamond and the square, and reciprocal may be used. The effects are more interesting when suggesting feathers or flower petals if the cuts are made quite freely without too much attention to regularity.

The top design illustrated is an angle cut into every other square, each point being raised away from the flat surface. If a closer design is desired, use every square, making sure that some paper is left around each angular opening, so it will not fall apart. The lower half of the same sheet shows a similar design using a semicircle instead of an angle. Gold paper was fastened to the back of the paper to give greater depth. Use a transparent or translucent paper if light is to come through.

In the lower rectangle four other combinations are suggested. The diagram below shows the line division of the surface to be changed. Experiment with your own ideas! New cuts will occur to you as you work. Remember, there must be background space left around each unit. Never lift out a piece of paper as you would in cutting a stencil. Cuts or slashes may be in opposition to each other or parallel. Curl or press away the free tab of paper leaving the opening exposed.

There is a line analysis for each of the abstract shapes. Use a free continuous swing when scoring the curved lines with a dull razor blade, for much depends upon the quality and sureness of the line. Thrust a corner through a slit in an opposite side and fasten securely. There is considerable pull or resistance in keeping these two ends together. The safest fastening is to take a strip of stiff paper, a short length, and slip this through a slit in the point that has been pushed through, to make a continuous curved form. Any variation of the curve or the number of scored lines gives an entirely new design.

The two upright units in either corner show the different planes in one shape, made possible with a few folds. In the four triangular shapes, curved parallel lines have been scored and pressed into position to show dark and light pattern.

By doing these elementary exercises the student learns the possibilities in manipulating paper to express ideas and to create designs that have as much art quality as those done in clay or plaster.

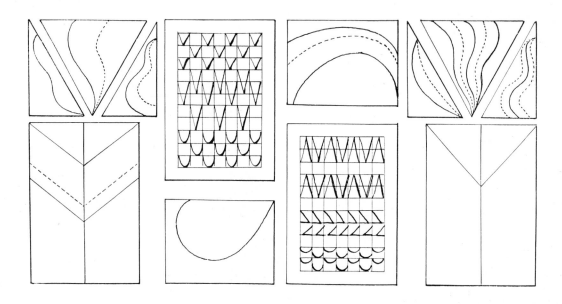

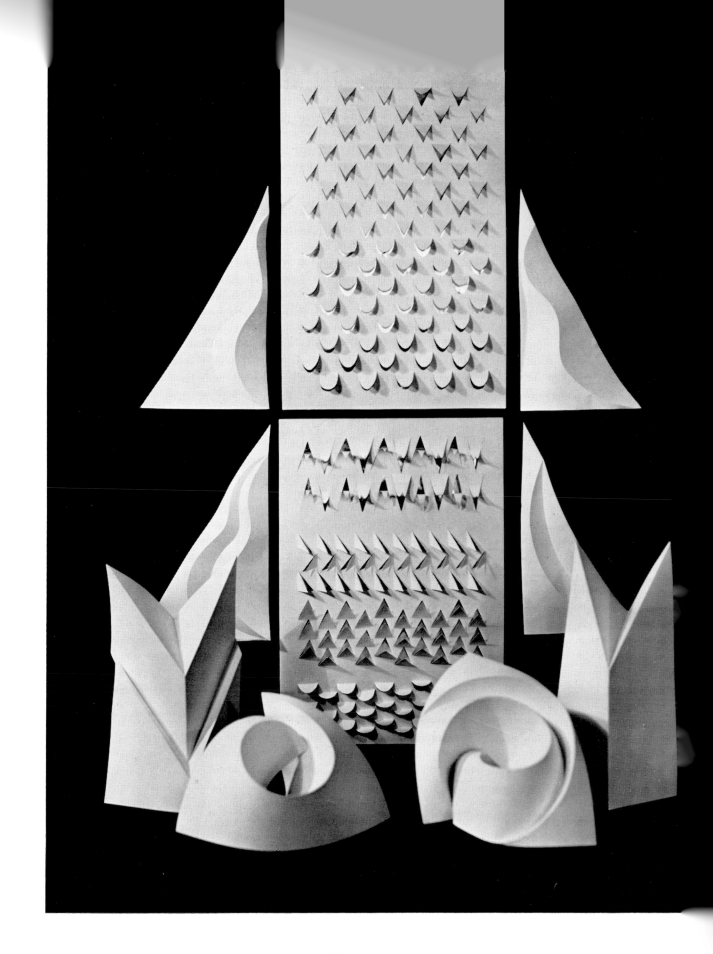

To Fix in Place with Strips of Paper

When there are a number of paper sculptured parts to be put together to form a design, the problem remains as to how to fasten one piece to another or to the background without disturbing the folds and rounded surfaces. The most practical and satisfactory method is to use fitted lifts or pads made of strips of paper.

Use a long strip of paper, the same color or value as the piece of paper on which it will rest. Cut off as many lengths as are needed to support one part of paper sculpture above another and keep the two separated. The folding and fastening together depends on the direction of the surfaces to which the lift is to be applied. Three suggestions are given in the diagram below. If a folded shape is to be fixed to a flat surface use a pad in the form of a triangle, one side against the flat part, the other two sides fitted against the sides of the fold. If one surface is curved and the background flat, fold the strip of paper twice, to result in a lift that will have one flat side and one curved side. A strip in a loop form will take care of two rounded parts, and a rectangular or boxlike pad will hold two flat pieces together. It is advisable to use at least three lifts of equal height to fasten in place any two parts of composition. This will also prevent shifting of any part of the design. Use paste, rubber cement or double-faced masking tape to attach the pads to the pieces of paper sculpture and to each other.

14

BASIC SHAPES AND FORMS

Cylinders

PAPER SCULPTURE begins when a flat piece of paper is curved or bent to produce more than a single plane. Fold a sheet of paper once and immediately you have two surfaces, one going away from you in space and one coming toward you. By curving and folding you create the effect of the third dimension.

The cylinder in all sizes and variations is the foundation form for paper sculpture in the round. The cylinder is easy to construct, structurally sound, and delightful to the eye; it should have a smooth, gently rounded surface and be completely circular at top and bottom.

Roll a sheet of paper, fasten at top and bottom and stand firmly on a flat surface so that the perfectly rounded, slender shape will support anything you wish to attach to it. If you want a fluted column use a length of paper at least twice as long as it is wide. Fold the long section once, then each half again, keep dividing each section in half with a fold until it becomes awkward to handle or the folds are twice as wide apart as you want the final pleat to be. Turn paper on the other side and score a line between each fold with a dull razor blade. Bend the length into accordion pleats and fasten together. For a cylinder with a recessed curved surface use paper from a roll or dampen a sheet of paper and roll it into the required shape, keeping it that way until it is dry. Score with a dull razor blade on the reverse side at regular intervals. Fasten the paper together against the natural curve. These curves may be manipulated until they are quite rounded. If they are laced together on the inside, they give the effect of deep shadowy folds. Examples of the modifications that can be made are shown on the opposite page. You'll refer to this section often because of the many uses cylinders have—as center support, rods, posts, pillars, columns, skirts, necks, heads, drums, etc.

In making any of these basic shapes or forms, the young artist will soon acquire skills and learn short cuts and methods that will aid him immeasurably in everything he attempts. For instance it has been found that in order to make a very slender rodlike cylinder, it is best to roll a rectangular sheet of paper, starting with a corner, around a knitting needle, a pencil, a dowel stick or the like, and let it set, first tying it in place with a bit of thread. On being released, the tightly curled paper will take a curved position and hold it. Then it can be rolled tighter, if need be, and fastened with glue or tape. For cylinders with a wider base, roll the paper to the size desired, tie and dampen slightly with steam or a wet cloth and allow to dry before removing the thread. The whole of the curved sheet may be used, cutting off each section as needed. When dealing with a wide, shallow cylinder, as with a drum, make a platform of a round cardboad plaque, or use a circular box top, to stretch the side of the cylinder around so that the top and bottom will be exactly circular.

In the photograph at the right are some open, curled cylinders that have been attached to other shapes. However, each one was the result of starting with the basic fundamentals described here. The success of the student's undertaking depends not only on his imaginative plan but also on his careful handling of the material and his willingness to take care with the basic geometric shapes or forms.

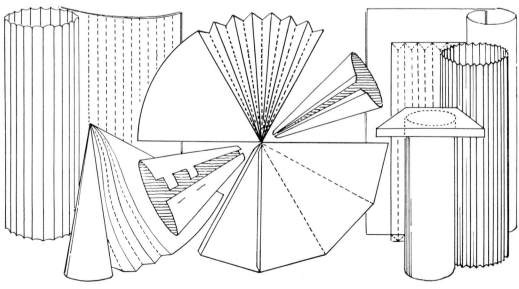

Cones

The circular cone shape is used to represent so many things in paper sculpture that it becomes a very important factor and must be constructed with knowledge and skill.

First, the cone must always be made of all or part of a true circular shape. If less than a whole disk is used, cut from the curved edge, to or through the exact center of the circular paper shape and back to the edge. Second, if the youngster is not yet ready to use a compass accurately, let him draw around a machine-cut circular plaque, or a carefully cutout heavy paper pattern. Third, find and use the exact true center of the circle. To find the center, fold the cutout circular paper pattern twice edge to edge, with the second fold at right angles to the first. Where the folds cross is the center. Lay the pattern on the paper, draw around it, insert a pin through the crisscrossed folds to the paper underneath, and the pattern has served as a compass.

In some instances the child will want the cone to come to a sharp, clean point. Using a semi-circular sheet of paper, he should find the center of the straight edge, then gently bend the paper back and forth at this point until it becomes limp and soft. When the half circle is folded into a cone, the point will be sharp. This technique is necessary only when the whole cone is used as in a clown's hat or a treetop.

Cone shapes vary from the almost flat to the very steep, thus giving a wide range for the child's originality in design.

If a tall slender cone shape is needed, it is wise to start with at least a half circle of paper, cutting off the excess after the shape of the cone has been determined. There is a photograph of this suggestion on the opposite page.

Cones may be made to fit, one into another. Use the same center point that was used in drawing the outside edge of the paper circle and draw a second circle with a much smaller radius. Cut the inside circular shape away. Any opening at the apex of the cone makes the construction of the cone much easier. Into this circular opening another smaller cone can be placed, point down. Draw a very light pencil line on the inserted cone around the edge where the two cones come together and from this line cut on three sides a couple of tabs which can be glued to the base cone, keeping the two cones quite stable.

Cones may be cut into or slashed to show a pattern of open areas, or scored and folded in either direction, to show deep grooves on the surface in concentric circles or to show graduated folds radiating out from the center to the edge. If a cone is to be pleated, use the whole circle and fold across the center making each crease the diameter.

To fasten the edges of the cone together, use glue along one edge, or pressure-sensitive tape overlapping one edge, or tack with a needle and thread in at least three places along the edge of one side. The edges might spring apart from the natural pull of the paper, unless care is taken to fasten permanently.

The student will find a greater degree of satisfaction in creating a fine shape or form that has stability and character, than he would if he did not heed these few suggestions.

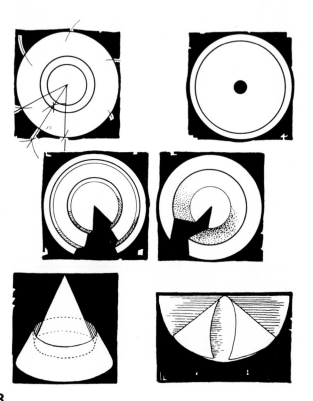

Abstractions

IN PAPER SCULPTURE, abstractions present an opportunity to escape from the concrete and deal in elements other than those of a material nature. On the opposite page are two examples of the plastic use of paper to create decorative form. These studies in paper sculpture show the transformation of a sheet of stiff paper into a spatial design of interweaving shapes by cutting, bending and compressing.

"Forms constructed geometrically are eternally beautiful," so the basic shapes should at all times be the square, the rectangle, the triangle and the circle. These shapes may be modified, overlapped or connected as the design grows. The rules and laws of rhythm, of proportion, of light values and full or empty space, should control the creation of abstract form.

It will prove more valuable to experiment with non-objective design than to produce commonplace realism.

It is essential to develop courage in the production of stimulating abstractions, whether they are for self-satisfaction or decoration.

Three-sided and four-sided pyramids are useful for supports, abstract designs and in the original form. Start with a whole circular shape, divide into the number of sides around the circumference, leave a lap for fastening, cut, fold and bring the sides together. If it is to be used as a part of an abstract unit it will need a base. Leave attached to one edge of the base, the square or triangle with lapping edges for attachment that is necessary to make the pyramid a solid shape.

An abstract decorative unit and a mobile are illustrated in the photograph on page 23. The mobile is composed of abstract forms suspended in space, with the added element of movement. Air currents rotate the mobile, creating constantly-changing visual patterns when seen from a fixed point of view. The stabile or wall ornament is a composition of positive and negative areas, which are ordered into well-defined space relationships. A strong direct light emphasizes the form as an element of space.

Abstract design in three dimensions is a most satisfying form of self-expression. In the diagram below are approximate outline drawings of the shapes that were used for the photographed paper-sculpture designs. These should serve only as suggestions for the initial shapes, not as patterns.

Each abstract form is of the spirit and creates for itself a new idea in form. The most acceptable and satisfactory designs are made in one piece, the balance of contrary forces and interweaving space is brought about by manipulation of the folds and edges of the paper. The diagram shows the outside and inside edges with the center line scored. The center does not have to be cut out, a slash on a reverse curve may serve.

The designs at the extreme left and right are made up of a pair of circular shapes. One pair is tangent, the other pair is connected with a bar. These are a very few of the many possible initial outlines—forms develop from simple shapes that have all the elements of beauty.

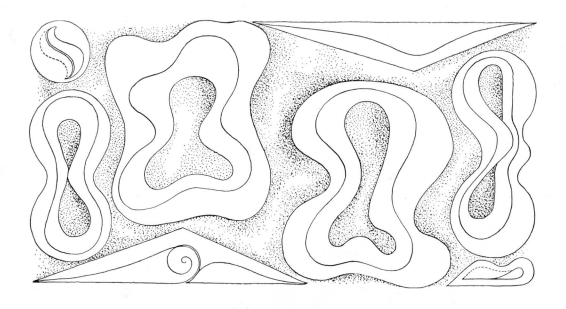

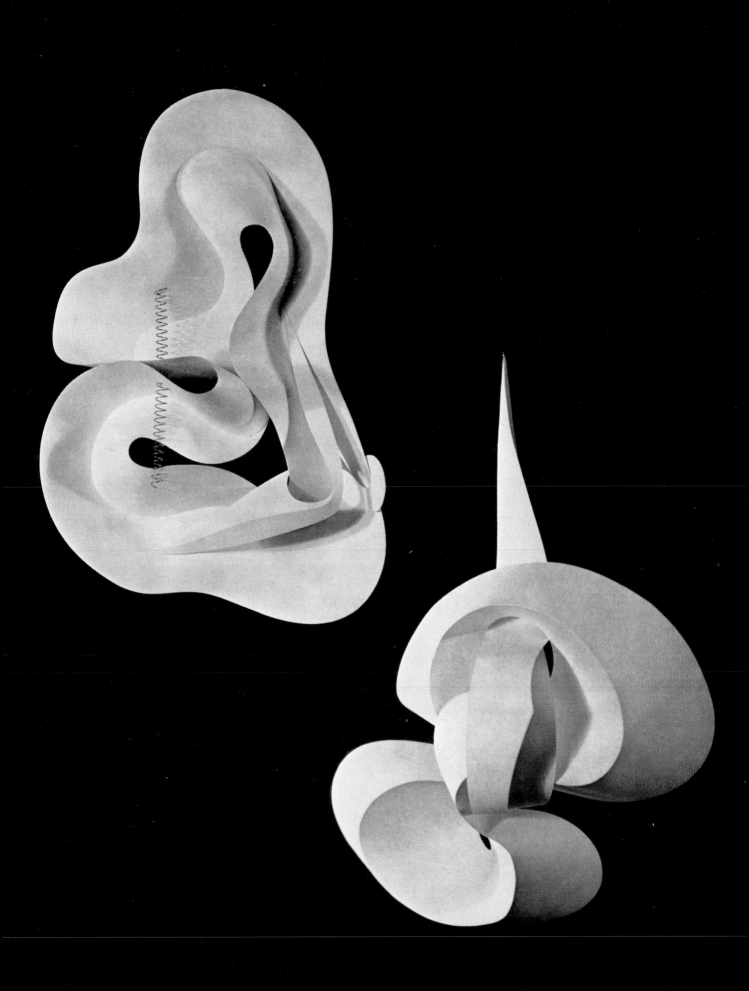

Geometric Forms

Geometric forms have several uses. All these shapes are interesting in the development of abstract design. Some designs in the round gain in interest if mounted on a rectangular solid platform or flat-topped pedestal. Careful measuring and right-angle corners are necessary if you wish these shapes to support anything or look right. Whether the idea is expressed in low relief, in high relief, or in the round it should be an honest effort to create original design.

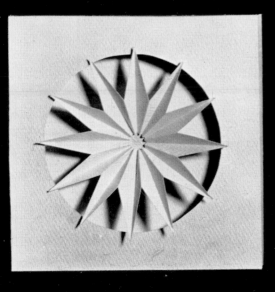
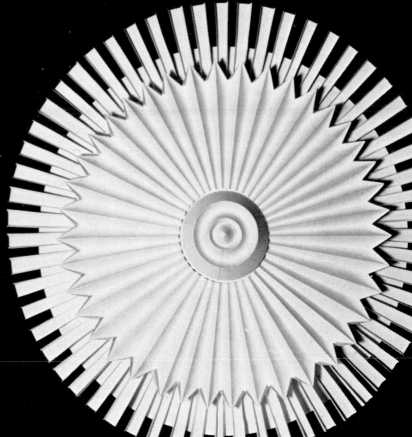

SPACE VEHICLES

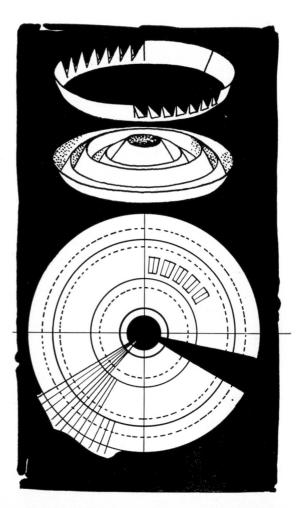

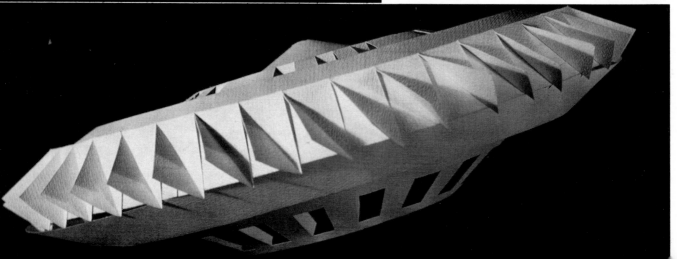

THE "SANTA MARIA"—COLUMBUS' FLAGSHIP

One of the first things we think of in relation to Christopher Columbus, whose birthday is celebrated in October, is the kind of ship he sailed in on his voyage to the new world. Every school child recognizes the general outline of the *Santa Maria,* the flagship of his fleet. Below on this page there is a photograph of a decoration done in paper sculpture of the same type of vessel. The illustration right shows the parts that went into the finished design. Both boys and girls will find exciting possibilities in reproducing in paper sculpture models of the famous ships in history. The line drawings of Roman galleys, Spanish galleons, British men-of-war and early American sailing ships that are in all history textbooks serve as inspiration for ship models for decorative purposes. At this stage of the child's development, an approximate characteristic shape should be sufficient; too much emphasis on exactness and accuracy may stifle his creativity. This problem will help develop judgment in space relationships.

In the photograph right, there are two cutout hulls, one lying flat, the other upright. The flat-surfaced one goes in back of the modeled one acting as a brace and a support. Before either of these was cut out, a simple line drawing was made, the size of the finished design. Each part, one at a time, was transferred to strong white paper in outline, cut from the sheet, then modeled and decorated. In the cutting, changes and variations of outline can be made, still keeping to the general size and proportion. Work on the essential basic part first, adding the masts, sails, rigging and decorations in this order.

Score and fold as many curved lines from stem to stern as desired; first on top, then on the back of the paper. Keep these lines apart but parallel, to suggest timbering. Score and fold all of these lines up to the curved line under the bow. The timbers hanging at the side, while they may be for ballast, create a pattern of light and shadow which adds to the interest of the design.

The masts are very slender, triangular shapes. They were scored and folded once, against a metal edge, so that they

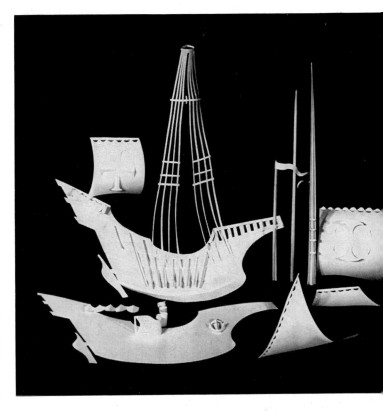

would be perfectly straight through the center. The mainmast was scored and folded twice again on either side of the center. With the paper folded as flat as possible, cut from base to tip, both sides at once, in a slender, tall, shaftlike triangular shape. The pennants flying from the mastheads are very long, triangular strips of paper, curled first in one direction, then in the opposite direction. Curve the wide end and attach to the masts billowing out in the breeze.

Use one long piece of paper for the rigging, cutting its length in very narrow strips. Leave all the fine lines attached at one end, fanning them out toward the bottom and bracing them with crosspieces. At the top attach to a loop which in turn is fixed to the mainmast.

Transfer the shapes of the sails to paper, making sure they are in a position to take the proper curve when the paper is rolled. This is important because, unless the ship model is on a small scale, the sails will be too large to curl between thumb and knife edge. Roll the paper in a loose curve, tie it, wrap it in damp paper and allow it to set. When the sails are thoroughly dry, cut out and decorate.

For the waves, take a full sheet of paper and divide it with pencil line horizontally into even strips or in progressively narrower strips than the first one. Divide vertically into even sections. Into alternate sections all over the paper, cut the two sides of a triangle as large as possible within the given space, the same two sides in each section. Curl from tip to base over the finger and against a knife blade.

In most instances the separate parts were fastened to the background or another part with small lifts made of paper as described on page 14. The ship was mounted on cardboard at the bottom edge so that it would appear in a vertical position. The sheet of waves lies flat on a table or shelf. If this decoration were mounted on a poster with lettering, the waves would be suggested from the bow back in a continuous curve or a series of curved wave shapes.

FLOWER FORMS

THE LESS REALISTIC flower shapes, in paper sculpture, have more interest and art quality than the ones that imitate nature too closely. Flower forms are used because there is a wealth of design material and inspiration in the structure of buds and blossoms. Reduced to the simplest form, all flowers are cone shaped. Some are so shallow they appear to be flat, others are quite deep. Study the structure of many flowers for inspiration in pure design. Cut a flower down through the center and note the exquisite space divisions. In paper sculpture, it is necessary to show form and pattern in dark and light in a manner that uses nature's inspiration but makes no attempt to copy or imitate.

The line drawing analysis below shows the shapes used to make the flower forms in the illustration. They should not be used as patterns. Ideas for new shapes will crop up as you cut and manipulate the paper—more satisfying in the end than following a pattern too closely.

As the basic shape is a cone, cut any number of circular shapes of varying sizes. For some flowers you will use the whole circle; for others, only part of the circle. Cut some of the shapes without using a compass. The slightly irregular shapes are more interesting than the carefully cut ones. If you cut freely with a razor blade the edge will have more verve and quality than if you cut with the scissors.

The large center flower in the illustration suggests a daisy. Hung in space on an invisible thread against a dark background, it is very effective for display or decoration. It is built of two layers of petals with a covered center. Each petal is scored and pressed to give the effect of the third dimension. The center is a mass of curled cones made by twisting a small circular piece toward a center. Any round flower, such as the poinsettia, the dahlia or the zinnia could be constructed after the same fashion.

For lily or tulip, use a semi-circle or less, or a triangle of paper, to cut out the basic shape. Build the cone first, then decide on the shape of the petal. Tulip shapes call for a cone with an even edge, some lilies are high on one side and low

on the opposite side. The line drawing below suggests several ways to cut the lily shape. Curl a long strip of paper into a spiral shape for the center. Fasten this way down in the cup before pulling the sides together.

For the flowers at the top of the illustration, start with a full circle scalloped around the edge. Cut in toward the center in a continuous spiral curve. The one with the shorter cut is scored through the center and folded. Keep twisting toward the center until you have a rosette. Fasten the ends in place and attach the whole to a background. These are quite conventional in design and resemble no particular flower but are excellent used in clusters with leaves for decoration.

Several layers of petals are used for those flower shapes that suggest the rose and gardenia. Cut square shapes the size desired, cut into center from each corner, leaving enough space to fasten to another square. Alternately curl one corner toward you—one away from you. Place several squares together with petals overlapping and fasten through a tightly curled centerpiece.

A simple shape with a nice sculptured feeling starts with a complete circle. Cut out, from edge to center, a wedge of about thirty degrees. Score in concentric circles, first on one side, then on the other, fold, cut petal scallops around the edge. Bring the cut sides together, overlap and fasten.

To get an edge to curl back away from a cup center, cut in toward the center in a quarter curve direction. Keep all cuts parallel to the first one and quite close together. Gently curve this fringe with a dull knife blade along the curve. When you fasten the sides of the cone together, the fringe will curve in reverse.

Use brilliantly colored paper for stage decoration and keep the design simple. Flowers and leaves should be cut on a larger than natural scale. They may be fastened together with staples for they do not show beyond a few feet. If flowers are used on posters or on hats for trimming, be sure to conceal the fastening or attach by using tabs which slip through slits in the background. In using flowers for decorations, above all, avoid elaborate or involved designs.

LEAF DECORATION

When the leaves fall in October, the ground is covered with some of nature's best structural designs and line patterns. No two leaves, even from the same tree branch, are alike; each is an example of fine design. Decorations, using a leaf motif, that have assumed a three-dimensional quality through cutting, scoring and folding are most effective. They may be stylized and used as conventional decoration, or they can be modeled in a realistic manner for factual display. The actual construction of leaves and plant forms in paper sculpture ought to be of value to the botany student. It is quite possible to create with paper the proportions and divisions of a true specimen. On the other hand, to the creative artist the shapes of leaves suggest many other stylized shapes.

School libraries have illustrated books showing line drawings of every leaf that grows. Study these drawings and if your decoration requires many, many leaves, figure a way to cut the leaves out in clusters or as many as possible at one time. Leaves may be used singly, in continuous vines, in garlands or in wreaths. They are simple to model and very satisfactory to see.

The leaves in the illustration belong to the elm, the oak, the horse chestnut, the maple, the ash and the holly tree. Each one is mounted separately on a sheet of nine-by-twelve white paper. Be careful to mount each leaf along its spine or at separate points so that it stands away from the background and casts a maximum of shadow.

32

SCROLL DESIGN

BIRD FORMS

The forms shown here do not imitate any particular birds, but suggest the soaring strength of birds in flight. Each of the forms except the one in the top center of the photograph is made from a single clean cut circular or triangular piece of paper. The one exception has a second triangular shape which is attached to the larger winged shape to suggest the rounded bird breast. In all the forms, scoring and folding makes the wing surfaces crisp and firm. Variation in designing these forms is natural and effortless.

The line drawing below shows a circular piece of paper, scored and folded through the center and cut as marked. Changes in plane or direction are made by scoring and folding the paper. The loose curved strip that partly edges the cutout shape was twisted over or under the body of the bird, and the folded end was passed through a slit in the folded center line. When the wings had been curved sufficiently, the end of the strip was fastened. The long slender neck and head section may be folded to point down or up. In this design the wings are symmetrical.

Another bird shape starts with a long narrow triangular piece of paper. This design will benefit if the wings are not symmetrical but cut freely with one side straight, the other slightly curved. The head and tail of the bird are cut from a second triangular area that has been left at the approximate center of the long thin triangular shape. Score and fold on a slightly reversed curved line from wing tip to wing tip, now score and fold from tip of second triangle or beak, back through the base of the triangle or tail. From here on, the child will know what more needs to be done. This is a very simple bird shape and most effective.

Another bird shape may be cut from the fold which will hold both sides together at the breast. Two heads are cut at once, two wings, two bodies and tail feathers. Next cut a smaller triangular piece of paper large enough to cover the breast part and under part of the bird. Curve the surface of the triangular shape over a knife blade and insert the two points of the three-cornered piece of paper, one on either side of the bird, cut out under the wing.

It is unnecessary to be realistic in cutting out bird shapes; it is enough if the outline suggests something flying **34** through space.

Turkey Gobbler

A strutting turkey gobbler with his tail feathers spread is a sight to see. His characteristic shape and form, the pattern of the various kinds of feathers he wears, make him most decorative. Modeling him in paper is a simple but exciting task.

Draw the whole bird divided into its sections as large as you wish, in pencil outline, on a single sheet of paper. Cut out the whole shape and make it the basis for the sculptured design. The turkey in the illustration measures overall about 30 by 32 inches; the basic shape underneath measures less.

In the illustration, the head and neck, the wattles, the breast, back and tail feathers, and the legs are separate pieces cut, folded and placed in position on the underbody. The parts are fastened to the foundation with small paper lifts, described on page 14, so that each section will cast a shadow. The body and tail feathers are parts of circular shapes. Cutting true disks and modifying them to suit the purpose is a good way to start. For a bright eye with expression, cut not quite around two or three concentric circles, and bend one in, the other out.

The photograph shows clearly how each kind of feather is cut and folded. There are other ways of creating a like effect, and the young artist, using his imagination, will produce something completely his own without imitation. Part of the pleasure in modeling in paper comes in figuring out for one's self ways and methods of creating the most effective form for the design.

When the sculptured turkey cock is complete, mount it so that it rests at least a half inch away from the background.

Cock—Weathervane

An early American, heavy iron weathervane suggested the paper sculptured cock in the illustration. This decoration is modeled in low relief of strong white paper against a dark cardboard panel. It is equally effective when it is done in full color and mounted on a wire-mesh background. It can be designed on a small scale to decorate a bulletin board or so large that it will dominate a room. The young student should plan the design in a small line drawing, from which he can deviate at will, as the decoration develops. The child, without conscious effort, will create fine pattern of light and dark in simplifying and stylizing the feather pattern of the barnyard bird. A clear photograph of a strutting cock is a help in organizing the first layout drawing. Take liberties with the outlines and divisions of space only after the child has learned something of the structure of the fowl. The larger the design the more freely and directly the young person will work.

The cock in the photograph has six parts. The head, neck and body are of one piece of paper. There are three groups of feathers; one for the cock's comb, and two for the flowing tail feathers. The two leg shapes are cut out and modeled separately. The line drawing of the bird prepared in advance is mainly to establish the size and proportion of the form to be modeled. This drawing can either be cut apart and used as a starting pattern, or it can be transferred in sections to the paper from which it is to be modeled. Drawing directly on the good paper is for those students who are skillful and experienced. None of the pencil marks will show if the drawing is done on the side of the paper opposite to that which will be the face of the design. Let the outline of the cock's shape be free-flowing and smooth, basing as many of the parts as possible on geometric shapes.

In cutting out the parts, younger children should use scissors, but a cleaner, more forceful line results from the use of a sharp knife or a razor blade. The slits and slashes for the feathered pattern must be made with the point of a very sharp instrument. A curved cut calls for more care and caution than one that is made with straight gashes. Remember to be temperate in the use of reverse curves, either cut or scored and folded.

Score and fold the directional lines in the cock's comb, wattles and tail feathers before separating the ends or cutting the feather tips into tapered points.

Join the several parts with small, flexible lifts of paper. When completed, fasten the decoration to a background panel in a raised position. Here again use paper pads and lifts to hold the modeled paper design in place.

36

DECORATIVE FISH

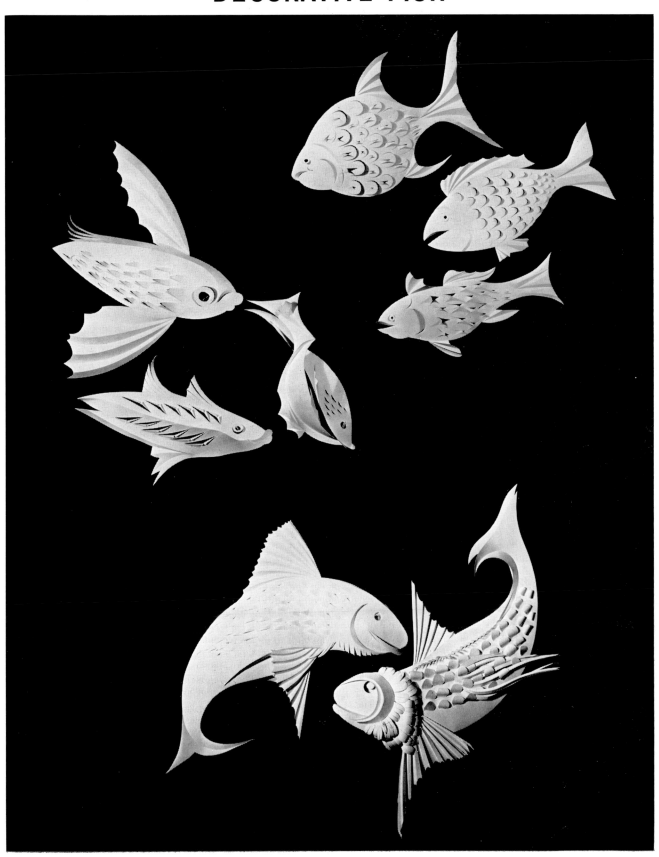

ANIMALS

French Poodle

Dogs have been modeled in papier-mâché for commercial display purposes for many years. They can be done in paper sculpture just as effectively, and with a greater degree of design quality. The French poodle in the illustration is an example of what can be done with a few sheets of strong paper. This model is deceptive in that it appears to be an elaborate piece of paper sculpture, too difficult for the in-

experienced hands of a beginner. On the contrary, it is composed only of paper, modeled into cones and curls, both of which the youngest artist can manage satisfactorily. The child may need help in assembling the various parts, but this poodle is one of those problems in design where a group may work together to create one piece of paper sculpture.

The basic structure of this and other animal forms is a series of differently proportioned paper cones. On page 18 are suggestions for many cone constructions. These cones are put together in various ways to form different types of animals.

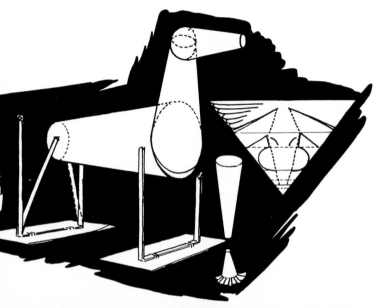

When finished, the animal must stand firmly on its four feet without wobbling or tilting. Therefore it will be wise to build something in the way of a support through the legs to carry the weight of the body. The framework for the French poodle dog is shown in the line drawing to the left as is the construction of the animal form itself. The foreleg brace and the hind leg brace may be fastened to separate bases, so that the position of the standing animal may be shifted about to give the design more vitality.

This particular breed of dog was chosen to illustrate the modeling of a four-legged animal, because the popular trim of a French poodle allows for bunches of curly hair to cover and disguise the joining of the several sized cones. It is very practical, always, to encourage the child to make an animal that has a rough and hairy coat.

The framework for the four legs, as shown in the diagram, will determine the size of the poodle. From here on, everything will be in proportion to the length of the legs. Four cones make up the forelegs. The back legs are the result of rolling two long strips of paper of equal length, cut from the circumference of a large circular sheet. Roll each long piece of paper in opposite directions, until there are two tight rolls of paper about the size or thickness the hind legs should be. Tie these in position and allow to stand over night, so that the dampness in the air will fix the curve. Untie, and slip one curl over each rear leg support allowing it to uncurl in an easy natural position. When the body part is in position the upper end of the strip can be fastened to the narrow edge of the cone.

Let the group or class cut and curl the circular pieces of paper that will become the bushy, curly shapes of the French poodle. It would take one child too long to cut and curl enough shapes to cover the desired parts. All of the curls start as circular shapes of paper, but two kinds of cuts were used here to show tight curls and long curls. The size of the round shape may vary from very small to medium large, and so will the cut, but manage to get two of each exactly alike so that one may be placed on each side, at the same time, thus making certain of a symmetrical form.

Cut two circular shapes of paper at one time with the scissors. Cut through to the center, and cut out a center circular section. This opening will allow the designer to do many things to one string of curls. They may be applied to the body of the animal in a circular position; they may be folded back in half; they may be cut into sections; or they may be curled around a form and fastened at the ends. Rubber cement has proved to be the best adhesive agent for applying the curls to the body or to one another. Put rubber cement on both surfaces, allow to dry, then gently press the two coated surfaces together.

The cut and curled semi-circular pieces of paper that become the nose, eyes, brow, ears and whiskers are outlined in the diagram. Each part starts as a quarter or half circular shape, and is modeled to suggest one of the dog's features. A small pert bow is placed in front of the top knot to complete the picture.

38

Lion and Lamb

It has been said that the month of March roars in like a lion and leaves peacefully as a lamb. In an association of ideas the two animals in the illustration are used to demonstrate the effectiveness of paper sculptured decorations. These are by no means the only animal forms that can be modeled in paper. Every animal in Noah's Ark presents a constructive and fascinating problem to the creative child. The study of

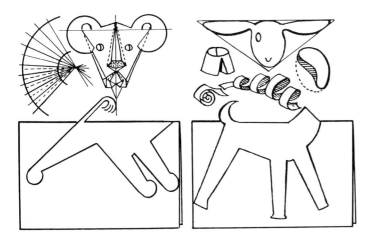

animal form serves as an impetus to original structural design, and as an expression of the child's imaginative and whimsical fantasies. The lion and the lamb in the photograph are modeled in low relief with a deliberate evasion of realism.

A front elevation or an almost profile view of the animal is most satisfactory when modeling in paper. Reduce the chosen animal shape to its simplest basic proportions and draw it in outline on heavy paper. Cut out the shape and use for either a foundation or a pattern. The placing of one modeled part over another creates an illusion of depth and solidity. Choose one salient characteristic in each animal form to emphasize and exaggerate, such as the ruff in the lion and the curly coat of the lamb. In modeling the parts, eliminate all but the essential patterns. Fit as many parts as possible of the animal structure into rectangular, circular or triangular shapes as shown in the diagram. Use a straight edge in preference to a curved edge, but if a curve is needed, use a part of a true circle. Avoid frequent and indecisive changes in direction; use parallel lines and right angles to make the design decisive and dramatic.

On this page there is a line analysis of the lion's head and ruff. Although the head is modeled to give it form, it is basically a triangular shape, with circular shapes on two of the angles for ears. The ruff is made of a complete circular shape with the fold lines passing through a center point.

Cut out the body of the lion on a fold. There will be six legs on the final cutout shape. Leave the two identical hind legs to be scored and folded to show thickness. Keep the near foreleg, but cut off the far foreleg. On the under section leave the far foreleg, but cut off the near front leg. Keep the two sides apart with a pad of paper to suggest thickness. Fasten the head to the ruff with fitted pads and the ruff to the body, so that there is enough space in between each part to cast a shadow. Different kinds of paper pads and lifts are shown on page 14.

The gamboling lamb is constructed in much the same way as the lion. Draw on the lower half of a sheet of paper the outline of the lamb's body without the head. Cut around the short tail, then fold the paper against the line of the backbone. Then cut through the two thicknesses of paper with scissors. Cut off the extra leg shapes in the same manner as the lion, but leave a rounded chest line from the near foreleg to the neck. For the head use a triangular piece of paper large enough to include the ear shapes. The head is cut and modeled separately. It is fastened to the body after the curls are applied. The drawing on this page suggests a way to develop a lamb's head, based on geometric shapes. Each curl of the woolly coat is a strip of paper curled over a dull knife blade, and recurled tightly between thumb and forefinger. Make many short slashes in the surface of the animal shape and insert into each an end of a curled strip of paper. To prevent the curls from slipping out of the cuts, fasten the ends to the back of the shape with small strips of pressure-sensitive tape. The hooves are cut from a slightly curved band of paper and fitted to the end of each leg. There is a slash in the center of each hoof to show a cleft. One side of the cut is scored and folded back.

Animals modeled in low relief like the lion and the lamb can be used as a decorative frieze around a classroom. They can be done in colored construction paper as well as in heavy, white drawing paper. Raise the modeled form away from its background with several small lifts or pads of paper. Tack the cardboard mount to horizontal strips of wood if it is to be hung against a wall.

39

Reindeer

Christmas reindeer prancing across a school bulletin board provide seasonal decoration that is sure to please. If the child's fancy demands a more realistic animal, it is possible to use this same approach with equal success.

The reindeer in the photograph might be called variations on a circle. With the compass draw a semi-circle in the lower part of a sheet of paper. This will be the upper edge of the foreleg, the back and the hind leg. Move the point of the compass up toward the curved line, and with a much smaller radius, swing a circular line around inside the semi-circle. Score and fold on this line for the center of the lower foreleg, the underneath part and the center of the hind leg. On the outside curve erect a right-angled triangle, tall enough so that when the pointed end is cut off there will be space enough to take care of the neck and head of the deer. The vertical edge of the triangle is toward the front, the slanted edge runs into the back of the design. The narrow end of the triangle is folded forward and cut to suggest the long deer head. Before cutting, draw the ear shapes on either side of the neck at the point where the fold will be, and the short tail shape at the end of the back.

For the antlers, start with a complete circle, on either side of which, draw curved lines. The photograph shows where the paper is to be scored and folded to create feeling of depth.

When designing two or more reindeer of the same size, work on all at the same time, using the same radii for the circular lines. No two will ever be exactly alike, for it is the free swinging lines that give the designs character. The compass lines are used only as a starting point.

Fix the antlers above the ears so that they tilt forward. Pressure-sensitive tape will hold them in place. Mount each reindeer so that it stands away from the background and casts its own shadow.

40

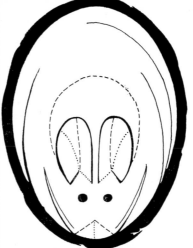

Mouse

Rocking Horse

Unrealistic and purely imaginative, the hobby horse is an excellent subject for decoration. Modeled in paper it is extremely ornamental. The design shown in the illustration is something between a merry-go-round steed and a hero's mount, fixed to rockers to suggest a toy. It should be drawn and modeled freely without constraint, and with imagination. Then it may be caparisoned with elaborate and glittering trappings. This type of paper sculpture gives the young student an opportunity to exercise his creativity fully.

Pattern in dark and light shows up best when the rocking horse is modeled in white paper, but young children may find colored construction paper more appealing. To attract greater attention to school advertisements and posters use brilliant foil papers to point up and trim the bridle, collar, and saddle. The rocking horse motif is useful in connection with the school circus, fair, parties and games.

A section of a narrow circular rim, scored and folded to represent a double rocker, supports and finishes the rocking horse.

Rabbit

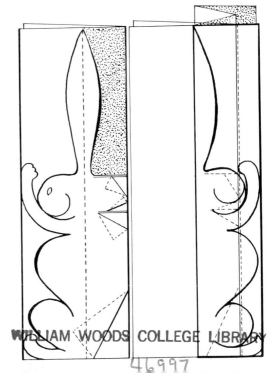

SYMBOLS

For an Exhibition

It was decided to use the Zodiac theme for seven large wall panels at a recent exhibition of paper sculpture at the New York Studio of the American Crayon Company. Reference was made to illustrated books on astronomy, almanacs, and old and new decorative maps.

Here was an opportunity to show how fine paper can be used and manipulated to express all kinds of shapes and forms. The ancient astronomers saw the constellations enveloped in, and in relation to familiar natural shapes, such as birds, fish, human form and animal form.

On page 37 in the lower part of the page, two fish representing PISCES, seen in the skies about November 10. On page 42 CAPRICORNUS (The Goat) to be seen about September 20 and LEO (The Lion) to be seen about April 10. On page 44 TAURUS (The Bull) to be seen about January 15. On page 45 SAGITTARIUS (The Archer) to be seen about August 20. On page 43 GEMINI (The Twins) to be seen about February 20 and VIRGO (The Virgin) to be seen about May 25.

The Zodiac is a belt of twelve constellations, seven of which have been interpreted in paper sculpture in this book, leaving Aries, Cancer, Libra, Scorpius, and Aquarius to be designed by students with experience in three-dimensional paper sculpture.

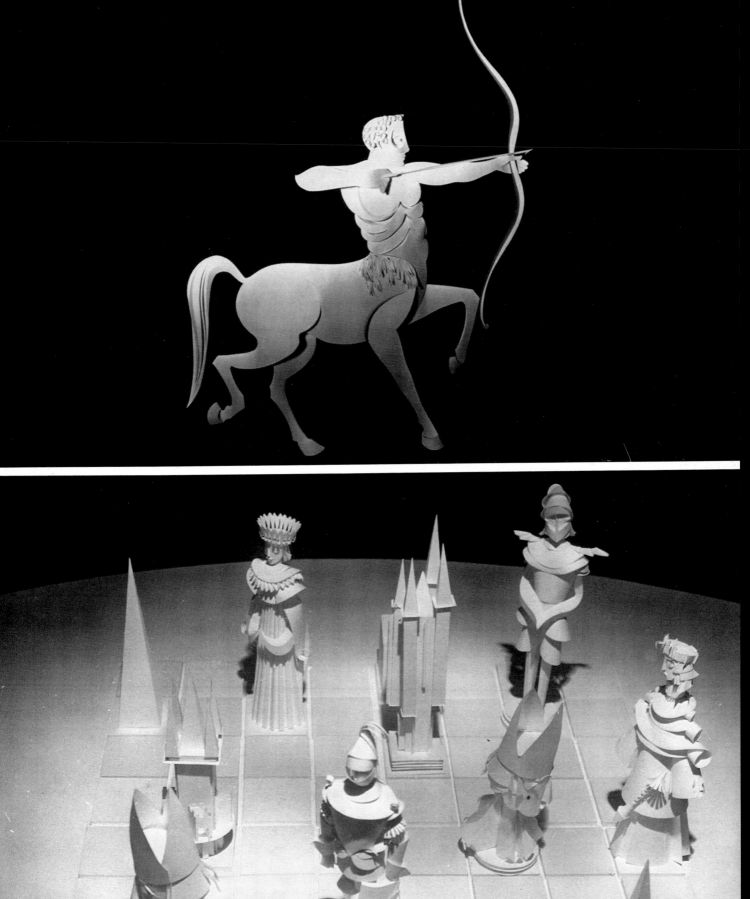

The Star Spangled Banner

The national emblem seems a fitting introduction to the following pages of suggested paper sculptured decorations that can be redesigned and made by children for use in the schools. Let this first example be in the nature of a salute to the Flag.

Two pieces of paper were used to complete the decoration that appears in the photograph below, one long narrow strip for the shaft and the largest piece available for the flag. Make the flag as large as possible—large stars are easier to draw and cut out.

The official proportion of the flag is one unit in height to one and nine-tenths units in length. The length of a fluttering, waving flag will measure about a quarter less than two times its height or width.

The size of the field in the flag decoration will determine the size of the whole flag. Starting near the upper left-hand corner of the large sheet of paper, held in a horizontal position, measure off forty-eight equal squares, eight across and six down. This is the field. Continue the horizontal, parallel lines the length of the paper; this will provide for six of the thirteen stripes. From the extreme left, under the field, measure for seven more stripes the full length of the paper. The width of each stripe is the same as the width of each square. Now check and see if the whole flag can be about one and three-quarters as long as it is high and still be within the sheet of paper. If the lengthwise lines run off the edge of the paper start measuring again, starting with a smaller square. Do all the measuring and dividing with lightly penciled straight lines first. Then, starting with the middle division, redraw with a flowing curved line. Let all the other horizontal lines take the same curved direction equal distances apart. Cut out of paper a five-pointed star of the proper size. Draw around this star in each of the square spaces so that all of the stars will be the same size. Cut away, with a sharp blade, the star shapes, leaving clean open shapes, through which the light may come. Before cutting the alternate white stripes out and away, score, but do not fold the lines that will indicate the rippling folds in the flag. Score these curved lines as far apart as you wish the folds to be deep. Score first on the front, then on the back of the flag as many times as you wish; then when the white stripes of the flag have been cut away, press these folds into position.

The shaft is a long strip of paper which has been scored and folded lengthwise, against a metal straight edge, at least twice and sometimes three times for lateral strength. The spearhead at one end is a triangular shape left on one end when the shaft was cut out. This has been scored and folded to accommodate the folds in the shaft.

This flag makes an effective decoration when it is hung so that a light is behind it. It can also be mounted against an appropriate background, using lifts or elevators of paper to keep it away from the mount.

If colored paper is used, proceed as above with the red paper. Make the blue field separately. When both sections are complete, superimpose the blue field, cutting away the red rectangular shape under the blue last of all. Mount this flag against an all-white surface.

Harp

Musical instruments, whether they are fanciful or romantic, obsolete or actual, lend themselves well to modeling in paper. They not only make fine decorative design units, but they also are useful as stage properties in school dramatics, pageants and tableaux. The grace of line and beauty of form in the musical instrument transfer with little effort to the paper sculptured model.

Decorations for the seventeenth of March would be incomplete without the Irish harp which differs from the console harp in that it has two curved sides and one straight side. Like all harps it is basically a triangular shape. The Irish harp in the illustration follows the general lines of the famous "Galway" harp, more elaborately decorated than some of the other examples of the traditional instruments.

To model a harp somewhat like the design illustrated, draw in outline the complete shape on heavy paper. Make a cutout pattern of the drawing of the frame. On three separate pieces of paper draw around the edge of the pattern; on one sheet of paper draw in the strings. Make each string shape twice as wide as you wish it to show when the model is complete. There will be three layers of cutout paper in the harp design. The top piece of paper is scored, folded and cut to give a sculptured effect. The middle piece supplies the strings which show under the frame. The third cutout shape braces the parts, and strengthens the structure of the whole design. Cut the paper away from the strings last of all for the attachment is delicate and easily broken. When the narrow strips of paper for strings are scored through the center and folded back they keep a straight taut direction and add to the three-dimensional effect. Refinements and decorative detail may be added to the basic frame shape. Musical instruments are especially effective when modeled of heavy gold or silver foil paper. This heavyweight paper is used extensively in the display business and may be purchased by the yard in any store supplying the decorating display trade.

The shamrock is very like our clover leaf—three heart-shaped leaves attached to a single stem. Try scoring and folding the center lines of all three leaves converging into the center of the stem before cutting the shapes around the incised lines. This procedure is especially recommended for over-large shamrocks, where the shadowed center ridge line is important to the over-all design. Scoring and folding deep ridges into the centers of leaves and stem stiffens the design and keeps the parts in place so that it can be hung in space as decoration or fixed lightly to a wall panel. The three-petaled shamrock may be used alone or in clusters.

47

Musical Instruments

THERE ARE no better examples of fine functional design than musical instruments. Their form and line are as pleasing to the eye as the melody they produce is pleasing to the ear. Reduced to basic shapes, they lend themselves readily to interpretation in paper sculpture. It is a challenge to the ingenuity and inventiveness of the artist to construct a form as exquisite as a violin from sheets of heavy paper. There is satisfaction in approaching the fine proportions of a musical instrument and it is excellent exercise in good judgment.

The photograph on the opposite page represents a conventional grouping of musical instruments tied together with a knotted ribbon. The paper sculpture is in white upon a dark background. It is equally effective done in glittering gold-foil paper on white.

Analyze the instrument first, either in its original form or through photographs. Make some sketches in whole or in part, deciding on the size and shape of each part. The line drawing below gives a graphic analysis of several musical instruments.

For the violin, cut identical shapes for the front and back of the body, including the neck. Before going further, complete the top. Cut two wedge shapes, one the fret and the other the tailpiece. Score and press back on three sides so that both shapes are higher than the flat surface of the upper side. Fix these to the violin shape by concealed strips that pass through the top part to be fastened in place with scotch tape. The "F" clefs are cut out and it is between these two shapes that the bridge to hold the strings is erected. This is a wedge of paper in the proper shape with four round holes through which the strings pass. Where the neck joins the body and at the base of the tailpiece, there should be a double ridge of paper to hold the ends of the strings.

The sides of the violin consist of a long strip of paper the thickness of the instrument plus enough on each side to cut into a fringe of squares to turn back away from the strip that is to be the side. With a dull knife blade flex the paper strip, first on one side to make it curve, then on the other to make a curve in reverse. Do this until the sides take on the same shape as the violin. Attach the sides around the bottom shape. Put the top piece on after the strings are in place.

For strings, score against a metal ruler and fold the paper in a sharp, perfectly straight line. Cut a very narrow strip through two thicknesses of paper. This gives a strong, fine folded line for strings. Tie one end of each string in a knot to keep it in place at the ridge of the tailpiece, pass the string through the round hole in the bridge and continue it until it slips through the wedge at the neck to the peg.

There are various ways of manipulating the neck to give it the appearance of being arched. Cut a strip of paper as wide as the neck but longer, curl one end and pleat the other as shown in the diagram. The curl acts as a base for the scroll which is cut separately and fastened one on each side. Between the body of the violin and the scroll curve the strip to give the neck the desired arch.

The pegs are very small cylinders slashed at both ends on opposite sides. One end has a hollow, curved circular piece for the tip, slipped on; the other end slips over the edge of the neckpiece below the scroll.

When the upper face of the violin is complete, cement it in place over the lower section with sides. Use plenty of cement on the folded-over tabs so that no pressure is necessary to attach the two parts.

The mandolin is a simple arrangement of circular pieces, one with a long neck, with a curved side. The illusion of depth is obtained by raising each section a little above the other with small paper springs. The strings are made and placed in position in the same manner as in the violin.

The trumpets are long slender cones with a narrow rim at the end. These may be short or long, alone or in groups.

The horn is a combination of triangle and circle. The triangle is scored on three sides and folded back at the sides and forward at the bottom. The triangle continues into the circle and is cut from edge to center in a spiral. One scored curve at the inner side becomes the center fold of the spiral horn. When scored lines have been folded in place, the form takes new directions and can be arranged in several ways.

A circular rim makes an interesting ribbon pressed into folds and tied in knots.

Fasten the instruments to one another or to the background by strips of paper which have previously been attached to the back of each instrument. Leave the shapes different distances from the background, but fix firmly in place.

Staff and Musical Symbols

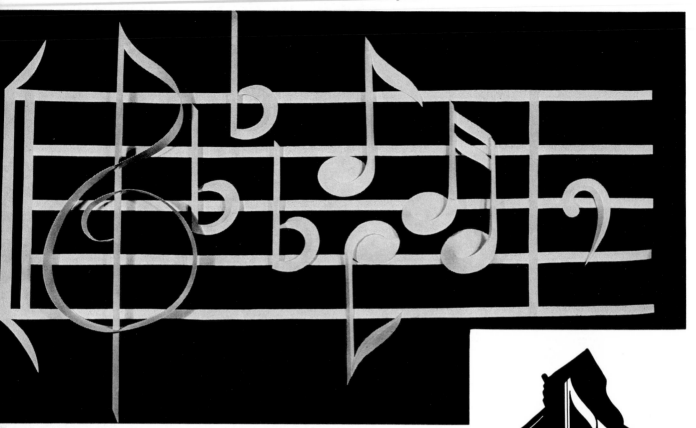

Library Books

Scout Insignia

The paper sculptured badge shown in the photograph is the identification of the Boy Scouts of America. Because it has meaning to American youth an effort has been made to model the shield, for decorative purposes, with dignity and accuracy. After considerable research, the small imprint on the cover of the Boy Scout Manual was found to be the best reference for detail and proportion. This type of ornament offers little leeway in original design, but it does present problems in representation, the solving of which will add immeasurably to the student's ability to interpret in a new medium an accepted arrangement of design elements.

As all of the parts of this design are bisymmetrical, with the exception of the wing sweep and eagle's head, they can be cut out from a center fold, both sides at once. These creased pieces of paper are the pattern parts. The finished badge calls for smooth, unbroken surfaces.

Draw and cut out two trefoil shapes peculiar to this particular design. When mounted one above the other the effect is of a beveled edge. Make a slit down through the center of the upper one, and score and press back on a line on either side of the cut to form a slender triangular depression. Place one fleur-de-lis shape over the other, fastening them together with paper pads so that there is an even space between them, and the smaller shape casts a shadow on the larger one. Model two five-pointed stars and fix these in place with small angle pads.

The eagle bearing the shield is composed of five layers of modeled paper, one over the other, raised slightly in position to give depth to the design.

Other badges, seals, and insignia can be modeled in paper to decorate for many different occasions. A three-dimensional symbol will catch and hold attention whenever it is used.

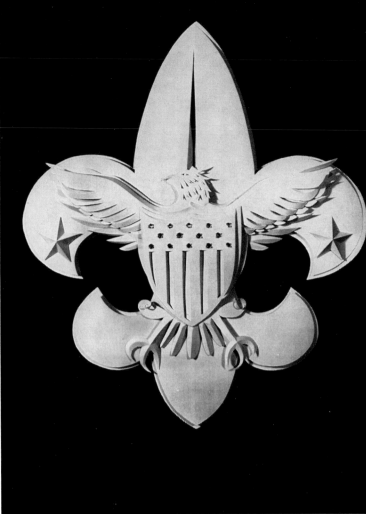

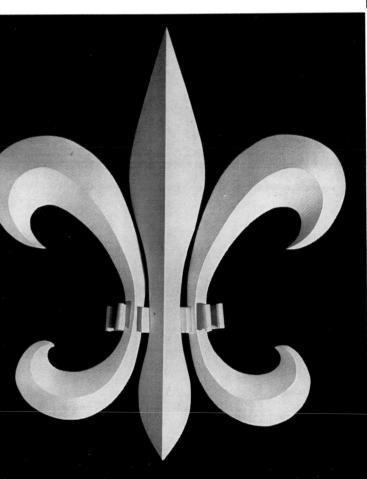

Fleur-De-Lis

Here is the way this fleur-de-lis was modeled. First the sheet was folded through the center lengthwise, then opened out flat again. The whole shape of the conventionalized lily was drawn very freely with the fold as a center. In this drawing three times as much space was left between the petals as finally appeared. This additional space is on the bar which holds the parts together. The drawing need not be entirely symmetrical because in the next step the paper is folded back on the crease and cut through the two thicknesses of paper with scissors. This cutout shape is the outline for as many fleur-de-lis as you want to model.

The direct, free-flowing curve through the center of each outside petal is vital to the design. After this curve had been drawn on the outline, one of the outside petals was cut along this curve so that the outside petals in the finished design could be scored symmetrically.

The half of the outline that had the complete outside petal was placed against the fold of a sheet of heavy paper and traced, so that the two halves of the design could be cut at one time. Then the shape was opened, and the side of the outline with the cutaway petal was used to draw the center line through each of the outside petals. On the same side of the paper as the center fold which had already been made, the curved lines through the centers of the outside petals were scored and folded, each curve opposite to the other. The paper was then turned over, and the band that holds the three sections together was scored and folded at the edge of each petal. Further scoring and folding of the band brought the three parts close together. The folded band was reinforced by a rectangular piece of paper attached behind it.

Drum

Sculptured in paper this drum will never make a sound but it will be noticed. It can be modeled so small it will serve as a party favor or it can be made actual size to carry in a parade. For purely decorative purposes it is best done in white paper, but for celebrations, tableaux and dramatic occasions it may be done in full color.

Reduced to its simplest form the drum is a solid cylinder. The entire construction consists of two long strips of paper, and two circular shapes or disks.

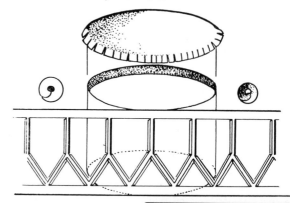

Trumpets

It presents less of a problem to model in paper a trumpet or horn five feet in length than it does to model one twelve inches long. The long one can be rolled from several sheets of paper, starting at the mouth tip with an extremely slender cornucopia, covering this with successive layers of paper, each one lengthening the original cone form. When the trumpet is long enough for its purpose an even edge will have to be cut with scissors at the widest end. To this edge, fasten a flaring circular rim. It may be necessary to experiment with this end piece until just the right degree of spread is obtained. If the edges of the paper used show enough to be objectionable, the whole trumpet, once it is modeled, may be covered with a cut and fitted single piece of paper. Gold foil paper or aluminum foil gives a satisfactory metallic cast to trumpets long or short.

The safest and most successful way to model trumpets to decorate posters or to be part of an heraldic design is to use a complete circular piece of paper for each trumpet. Cut through from edge to center on the radius. Begin folding one straight edge under the other until a tight cone is formed. Only a small sector of the circular piece of paper is necessary to produce a trumpet cone, but unless it is rolled first as directed, the edges of the cut shape will spring apart and make fastening the edges together a difficult matter, especially for children. Let the rolled cone stand a while until it sets in position. Then cut away a sector of the whole circular piece of paper, at least three times more than is needed to model a one-layer cone. Proceed with this piece, which is already curved in the direction in which it should go, rolling it tighter and tighter until it is very narrow at the tip, spreading gradually and slowly along the tube. An additional curved rim must be added to suggest the flaring bell at the mouth of the instrument.

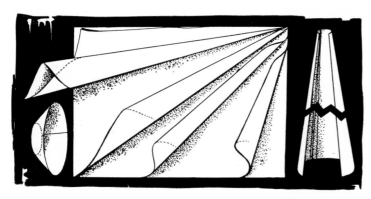

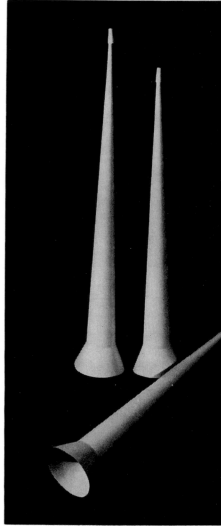

Anchor

As a symbol of things nautical, the paper sculptured anchor shown in the illustration can be used as an ornamental decoration wherever and whenever ships, sailors and Sea Scouts are concerned. This anchor was designed after the style of "Captain Kidd's," rather than in the Navy tradition, because the functionally designed Navy gear has little or no appeal to the child's imagination. The decorative anchor may be used as a unit, crossed with another as an emblem, or it may become part of a composition like a shield or seal. Other shapes related to sea travel such as the sextant, a ship's wheel, a round life preserver, crossed oars, and flying pennants can be modeled of paper and used to decorate for the same occasions.

There are a few directions that must be followed; then there is complete freedom of the individual to design a completely original anchor. The drawing below shows the lines that need to be made mechanically, and in proper relationship to one another.

Use all of a rectangular sheet of paper for this anchor. The dimensions of the paper will determine the size of the anchor decoration; the ring and shaft being its whole length, and the two hooks its width. Links of the chain may be fashioned from paper that will be cut away from the pattern.

A more interesting design will result when the shape that has been cut out lies flat and unfolded in the beginning. Therefore, it will be best to fold one piece of paper through the center the long way and cut two sides at once from the fold. Open out this cutout design and place it on a clean sheet of paper, drawing around it to transfer the design. Before cutting, true up the outline drawing, using a compass for the ring at the end of the shaft, and for the scored and folded center line of curved hooks.

The scoring and folding of the shape is responsible for the appearance of depth and solidity. It will be noticed in the photograph of the anchor, that the vertical center line has

been scored and folded only from below the cross-bar to the curved center line of the hooks. The smooth surface above and below the fold may be treated the way the child thinks best. Here the lines above the shaft have been scored and folded first on one side, then on the other side in oblique and horizontal directions. The two hooks have been modeled on continuous curved lines to a point, and where the curved line meets the shaft, an angle has been scored and folded on the back of the design.

For the heavy links of the anchor chain and the extra ring, draw three concentric circles a trifle larger than the ring should be; cut on the two outside circular lines and score and fold on the middle line, overlapping the cut ends of the rim to get a ring with two sides. When these rings are meant for a heavy chain, slip the open circlet through the closed ring before gluing the overlapping ends together.

53

FIGURES IN DESIGN

Standing Figure

A MOST SATISFACTORY SUBJECT for paper sculpture is the costumed figure. The one illustrated is "in the round"—completely finished on all sides—standing firmly without support. Historic costume plates offer inspiration for endless designs. Trousered legs can be managed but long-skirted figures are the simplest to construct. Anything over 24 inches needs a base and some sort of foundation structure of wire or wood. A wooden dowel centered in a block of wood with a crosspiece of wire at shoulder height is sufficient to keep a tall figure in position.

A Tanagra figurine suggested the figure in the illustration. Greek costumes, with folds and drapes, are rich in pattern and easily adapted to paper sculpture.

Decide the height of the figure to be constructed. Use the head, from top to chin, as a unit of measure and arrange for a figure eight heads tall. Figure the height in inches from the shoulder line to the hem line and cut out a length of paper, three or four times as long as it is high. Fold this length vertically into narrow reverse folds. Fold in half, then in half again, continuing to fold each section in half until it is impractical to fold further. Press tightly together so that each fold is straight and sharp. This forms the basic cylindrical shape for the skirt and bodice. At waistline level, cut out a slender diamond shape from every other fold. This opening should be on the outside when folded. Fasten into a cylinder with rubber cement or staples along the short ends. Stand the cylinder on its lower edge and tie a thread around the cutout waistline. Tighten until the waist is in the proper proportion. This ought to balance easily and stand alone. Pull out the lower edge until the skirt flares at the bottom.

Make a variety of folds and flying draperies, which may be fitted and fixed to the skirt. The illustration shows a draped peplum as well as side drapery and sweeping folds in the skirt.

The diagram at the bottom of the page shows how to cut, score and fold two types of drapery. Start with long narrow triangular shapes in the correct size. Fold with the center

point at the top in one instance and with the point below in the other. The position of point will determine the kind of drapery. Score first one side, turn over and score on that side, repeating until there is no more room. All these scored lines should converge at the point. Attach these to the skirt where the fastening will not show.

For the hip section use a circle of paper with the center cut out. This should be smooth for contrast and fastened tightly around the waistline. Remove the thread and use a narrow circular rim, curled as shown below, for a belt.

Cut out a pair of arms and hands following a curve. The scored line within this shape produces a fold which gives the impression of the third dimension. Fasten these at shoulder level so that the bend at the elbow is at waist level. The three semi-circular shapes of varying sizes suggest caps of a sleeve and should be fixed in the proper place around the arm. The breastplates are circular in shape, slashed at the center, overlapped and fastened by a tab. Fix these by attaching them to thin double strips which go through the waistline.

The head is constructed last. It should be one-eighth of the height of the whole figure. On a small head do little with the features, keep them simple and unimportant. The neck is a long thin cylinder. Attach the head, when complete, to the neck, leaving chin free and away. The shoulder piece, which is circular, should be wide enough to reach across both shoulders and cover the sleeves. Cut through the rim of the shoulders and fasten so it fits around the neck closely.

Cluster curls across the forehead, down the sides of the face and in back. Fill in the opening at the top of the head with tight curls made continuously as a fringe. The hair may be held in place with a thin paper strip for a ribbon.

When the head is complete with shoulders, push the long cylindrical neck down through the center of the structure toward the waistline. Tilt the head a little to one side for added grace. Arrange the hands in an easy position, giving them something to hold if necessary.

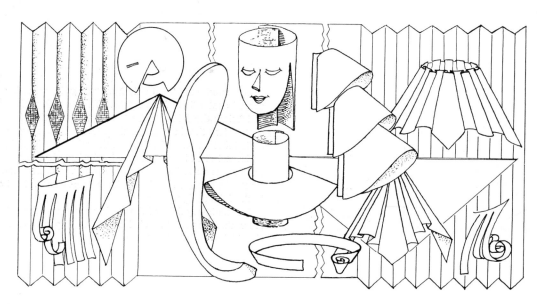

54

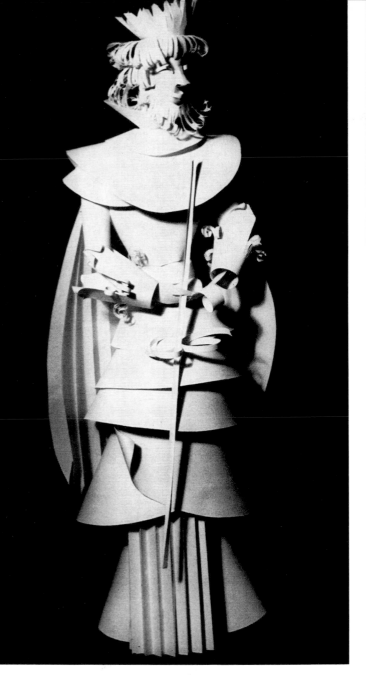

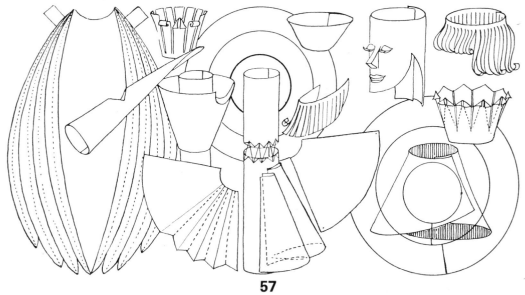

Carolers

Standing alone or in a procession the choirboy figure can add to the joy and gaiety of the holiday season. With a red cassock, white surplice, black hair and bow tie, he makes a beguiling color note in any Christmas decoration.

Start to design the figure with a circular piece of paper, the radius of which will determine the approximate height of the figure. Score and fold from the center point to a point on the circumference of this cutout circular piece, at even intervals. Turn the paper over and score and fold from the same center to a point midway between the folds already made. Press the alternate folds into place, and run a thread through the back fold of paper near the edge. Tie the thread ends tightly enough to have a tall, slender, pleated cone. This form reaches from the floor to the base of the neck, and is the foundation of the figure. It will stand firmly on a flat surface. Cut off the tip of the cone to allow a slender cylinder to be inserted for the neck which in turn supports the head.

Use two circular shapes of different sizes for the surplice and the collar. Cut a small circular opening in the center of each so that each part when it becomes a cone will slip over the cylinder that is the neck.

The sleeves are two triangular shapes, cut alike with a tab of paper left at one corner of each triangle for a hand shape. From corner to corner on opposite sides of the sleeve triangles, score a curved line, fold back and curve into position to give a rounded three-dimensional look to an otherwise flat shape. Curl the flat corners to increase the roundness. Fasten the top point on either side of the center of the cone which is the surplice with thread. Tie loosely so that the sleeve and hand can be arranged in various positions. The collar shape will cover the joining of the two parts.

Arrange for a slightly wider cylinder than the neck for the head shape, and cut a curved edge at top and bottom to suggest the forehead and chin. At the widest part of the head cylinder, cut an opening for the mouth and eyes. The hair consists of semi-circular shapes and round flat pieces of paper cut in fringes that are curled one way and lightly glued to the head to cover the top opening of the cylinder.

The head should be fastened to the neck with needle and thread so that it may be tilted in one of several directions. The hands, in place of the sheet of music, may hold tiny rolled taperlike cylinders to suggest tall candles.

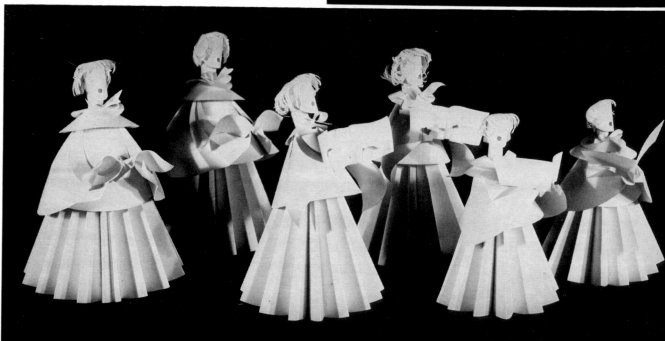

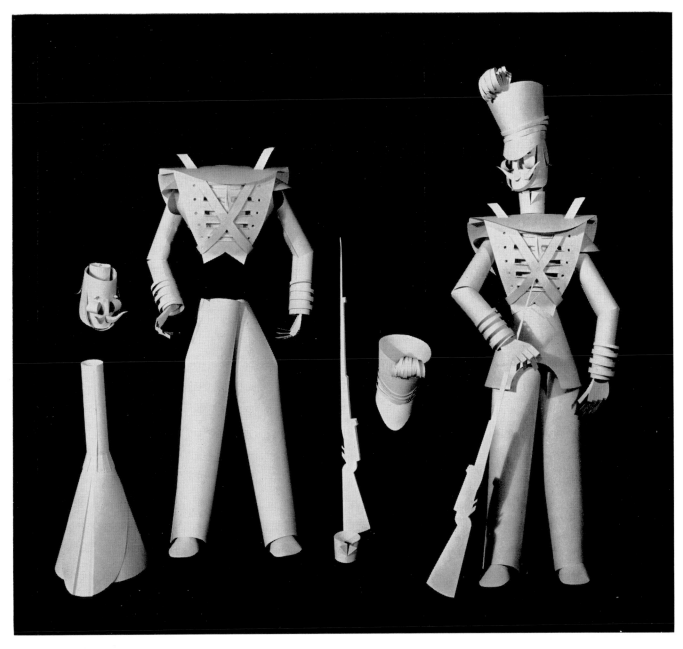

Toy Soldier

The military figure in the illustration is modeled in paper to stand at ease or at attention, or to stride ahead as if on parade. The toy soldier, belonging as he does to no particular time and story, has a constant appeal to all children. This kind of modeled figure may also be articulated and used as a puppet; then his joints must be hinged or threaded together, and he will be held up with threads instead of standing upright on a base. The several parts that go into the standing figure are shown in the photograph on this page, and it will be noticed that with few exceptions, the forms are paper cylinders and cones. Their relationship to one another as to size and proportion will present the only problem to the young artist in paper sculpture.

Let the student prepare a base, which in this instance is a heavy cardboard plaque, on which he can raise an upright slender cylinder or shaft, to pass through one shoe and trouser leg to support the figure to the waistline. The skirt of the coat, which is cut from a cone, is fastened to a slender cylinder the thickness of the neck. This form when placed over the cylindrical trouser legs supports the whole upper portion of the figure. The head and hat are tacked to the upper end of this same cylinder so that the head may be tilted in one of several directions.

It is suggested that all figures in the round be modeled in paper at least 18 inches tall, because on smaller constructions, the making and assembling of the parts may become tedious. A paper sculptured figure like the toy soldier in the illustration, based as it is on simple geometric forms, can be constructed life size, providing window width, seamless paper is available, and a strong supporting armature is used.

Old Testament Prophets

The treatment of the three biblical characters, Moses, Hosea, and Malachi, is contemporary in design and at the same time reminiscent of the stone carvings of the Middle Ages. They are in high relief attached lightly to a flat wall surface.

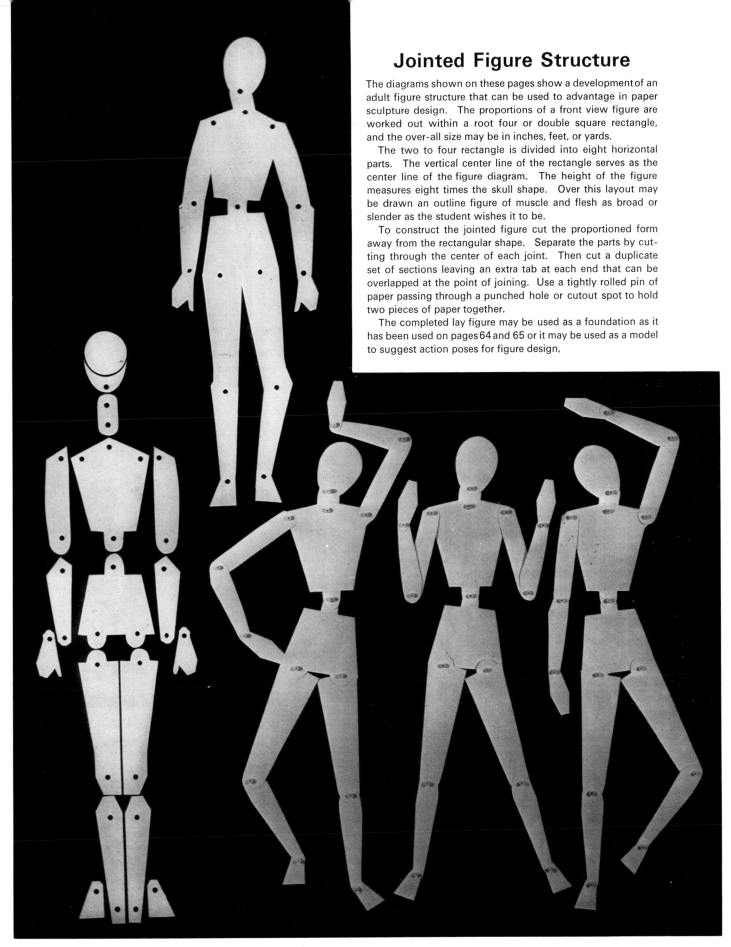

Jointed Figure Structure

The diagrams shown on these pages show a development of an adult figure structure that can be used to advantage in paper sculpture design. The proportions of a front view figure are worked out within a root four or double square rectangle, and the over-all size may be in inches, feet, or yards.

The two to four rectangle is divided into eight horizontal parts. The vertical center line of the rectangle serves as the center line of the figure diagram. The height of the figure measures eight times the skull shape. Over this layout may be drawn an outline figure of muscle and flesh as broad or slender as the student wishes it to be.

To construct the jointed figure cut the proportioned form away from the rectangular shape. Separate the parts by cutting through the center of each joint. Then cut a duplicate set of sections leaving an extra tab at each end that can be overlapped at the point of joining. Use a tightly rolled pin of paper passing through a punched hole or cutout spot to hold two pieces of paper together.

The completed lay figure may be used as a foundation as it has been used on pages 64 and 65 or it may be used as a model to suggest action poses for figure design.

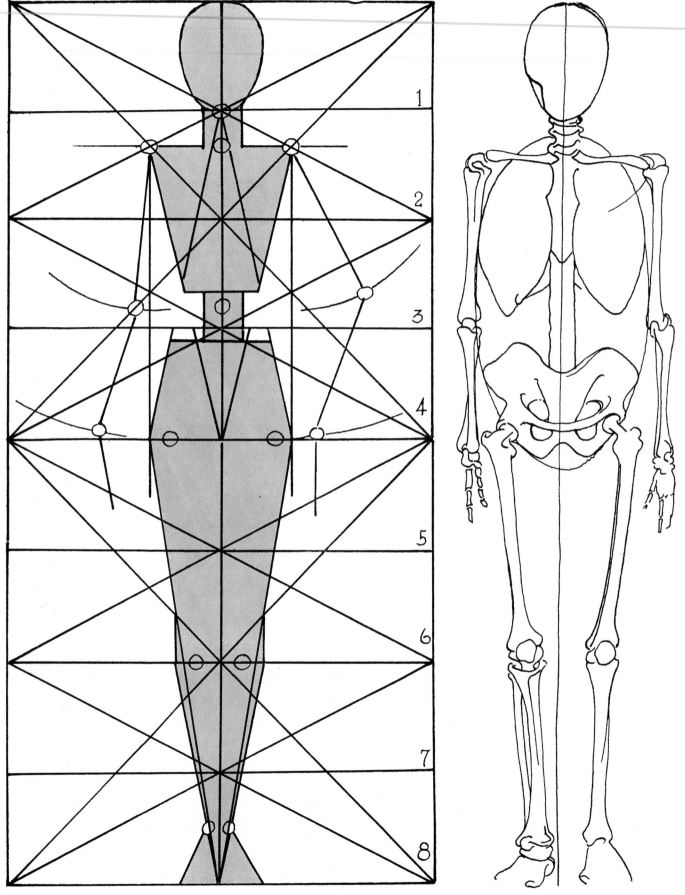

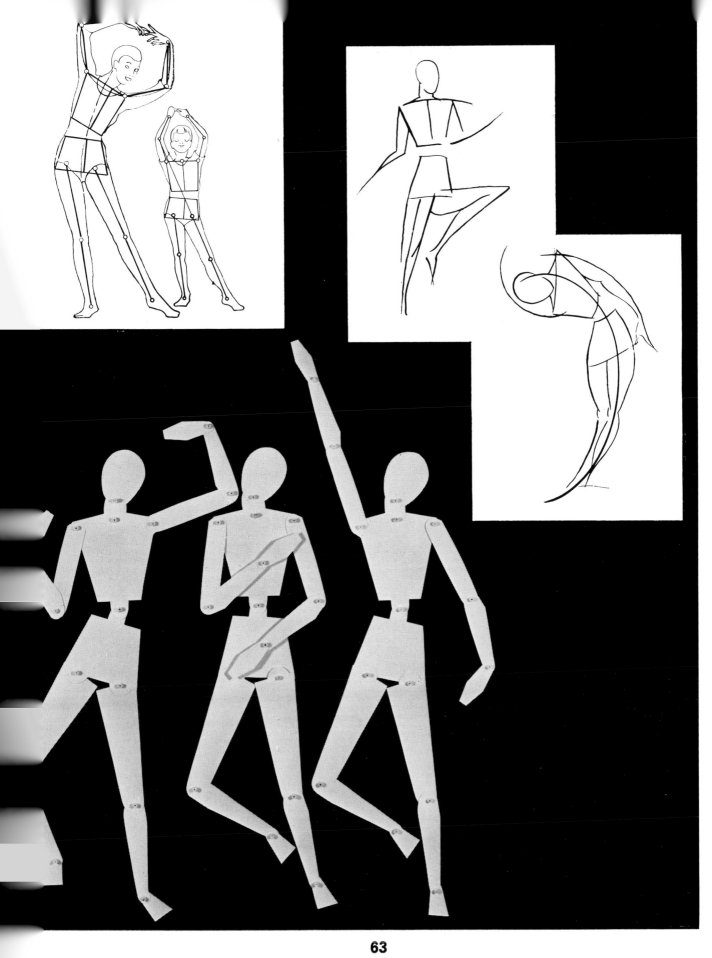

63

Costumed Figures

For serious research in period costume there is no better source than "The Book of Costume," by Millia Davenport. There are more than three thousand illustrations of people wearing the garments of their time and age. All are authentic because the particular record was made by a contemporary artist. This book is a splendid stimulus to the imagination.

In the illustration are six figures in action clothed in recognizable period costume; a wall painting in the tomb of Prince Amenkhopshef (1167 B.C.) suggested the cut of the clothes of the Egyptian; a small figure decorating a ceremonial cup (550 B.C.) was responsible for the draperies of the Greek warrior; a dancing figure on a vase called attention to the soft folds covering the Grecian woman; the Roman Praetorian wears a composite costume taken from several soldiers in a relief sculpture (11 A.D.); the man in armor is wearing a design that was popular in Italy (1460 A.D.); and the Flemish Dandy is attired in the court dress of his day (1550 A.D.).

Treat the figure and the dress in a conventional and decorative manner. Avoid realism and lean toward slight exaggerations in the over-all pattern.

The various costumes in the illustration were applied to articulated puppet figures and are in low relief. They may be modelled on a small scale or be life size.

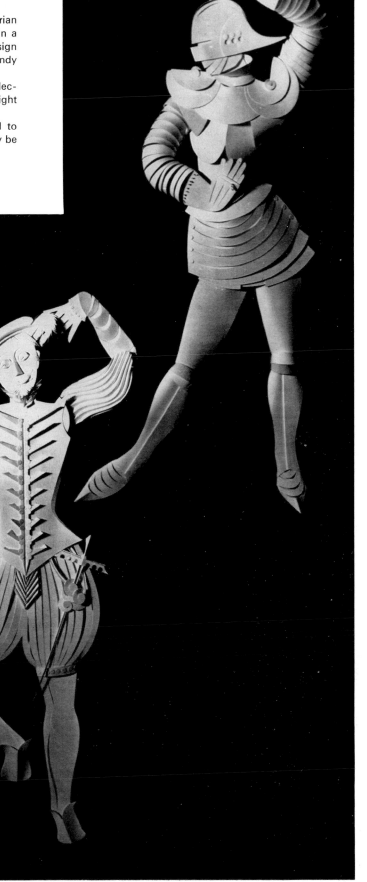

Clown

A circus clown modeled in paper can be a most attractive fellow, expressing all that is springlike, childlike and gay. It may be constructed with as many imaginative exaggerations as the child wishes. This clown stands firmly on his feet, but is flexible enough to move into several different positions. Except for the head, ruff and hands, he is constructed of variously modeled paper cones. Slight changes in the size or proportion of the parts create entirely new personalities for this comic figure of fun.

A tall, slender paper cylinder, which supports the clown, is first built. It is fastened with Scotch Brand Pressure-sensitive Tape at right angles to a cardboard base. Parts of the figure can be slipped over this cylindrical support and fixed at intervals in the proper positions. The cylinder reaches from the base up through the head and therefore will determine the height of the clown. If the cylinder is made just thick enough to serve as the clown's neck, no additional part will be needed to support the ruff, head, and hat.

The pantaloons are two tall cones of paper, scored and folded back in a circular line at the bottom edge to permit the flat, shallow paper cones to come out from under the trouser legs. These flat cones may be cut from a point beyond the center point and folded into place so that there appears

to be a pointed-toe shoe under each trouser leg. Tall, narrow cones are much easier to construct if they have been precurved. To do this, roll more of the circular shape than is intended to be used, even the whole of the shape into an overlapping tight cone. Fix it in position and tie it with thread by winding the thread around and around the cone form. Leave it in position over night or for several hours, releasing it when it has taken a curved position. Cut from this rolled, circular shape, two equal wedge shapes of paper for the two cones to represent the pantaloons. Fasten the edges together with Higgins Vegetable Glue, slip one cone over the upright shaft attached to the base, and then fasten the two leg cones together at the hip section.

The blouse or tunic is a pleated or fluted cone made of a whole circular shape. The bottom edge has been scored and folded to show thickness. Buttons down the front of the coat are small flat circular pieces of paper inserted into a sharply slanted cut on one center fold. Tack this pleated cone to the vertical center so that it will be in a position to support the sleeves and the shoulder cone.

Cut out the hands of two thicknesses of paper, leaving a length of wrist to go into a slit in a circular piece of paper. This disk should be slightly smaller than the opening at the end of the cone which makes the sleeve. The tight fit of this disk will hold the hand in the center of the sleeve and allow it to be moved into many different positions. The hand need not have fingers; it could be a mitten shape which could be curled about a hoop or similar object.

Neck ruffs like the one that the pictured clown is wearing are made of two or more curved lengths of paper cut from around the outside of circular shapes. Cut two or three identical rims of paper, fold each backward and forward in even pleats, run a needle and thread through the center of the narrow end of each fold, gathering the separate pleated rims into one continuous ruffle. Use the thread ends to tie the ruff around the neck.

Construct the head and tall hat as a unit, which will rest lightly on the upper end of the thin upright cylinder that supports the different parts of the figure. This paper sculptured clown is designed to be viewed from all angles, with all parts finished. The drawing on this page shows the details of the clown's features and hair.

Construct the hat as a tall pointed cone. Cut out a circular piece of paper with a radius equal to the proposed height of the hat. Score, but do not fold on the circumference of a slightly smaller circle with the same center. Make a slash from the outside circumference to the center point. Roll one edge under and continue to roll the paper into a tight cone until the tip is a sharp point and the curved edges around the circle are even. Leave the cone in this position until the curve is set, then cut away a sector of the circular shape of paper, big enough to fit the head of the clown. Fold back on the curved line that has already been scored for the brim or cuff of the hat, and fasten the edges together with glue. A small slender cone tends to gap at the point unless it is curled into place before it is cut out.

Schoolboy and Girl

Small figures modeled in low relief will prove to be one of the most popular motifs in design. At any age the child will want to use the human figure in his compositions. Those children who have an instinctive feeling for good proportion and an ability to represent an illustrative figure should make a simple line drawing first, using tissue tracing paper to transfer each part to the heavier paper before it is cut out. Each part is applied to a foundation of the entire figure, one on top of the other.

The two little figures in the illustration have been reduced to an almost diagrammatic formula so that anyone, without special knowledge, could create a reasonable image of a youngster in costume.

It will be best in this instance to establish first a foundation form upon which the child can design and build, as indicated in the diagram. When these parts are fastened together they form a basic shape that can be used to judge the size and shape of the clothes that are designed to cover it. The arms and legs will need to be shaped a little if they are to be left uncovered.

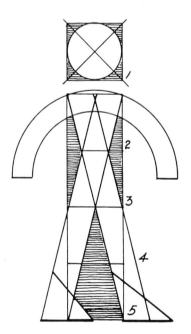

The boy and girl illustrated are about five heads tall, or five squares tall. Each separate and additional part like the hair, shirt, collar, trousers, blouse and skirt is cut to fit and outside the lines of the figure. The folds are made by scoring and folding, and the little girl's skirt is a section of a circular piece of paper that has been pleated in opposite directions from the center. Fold and curve the arms any way you wish. Attach the parts one to another with an almost flat pad of paper between, so that each part casts a shadow. Mount the figures on the poster or panel with enough space between the figure and the background to throw the boy and girl into relief.

HEADS AND MASKS

Girls' Heads—Side View

PAPER-SCULPTURED HEADS, in low relief, make an attractive complement to posters, signs, showcase displays and window decoration. Heads of every description may be used in this easy profile view with only one side of the face to consider. Historic characters with characteristic features and hair arrangements are simple to represent. Exaggeration of a dominant nose, lip or chin creates a head in caricature, or you can design a pretty girl's head or a manly boy's head with equal ease.

When hands are used be sure they are in proportion to the head. One way to be sure of this is to make the head life-size and use an actual hand for a pattern.

The lettering on a poster should also be in relief. Either cut out each letter or use commercially cut alphabets for slogans and directions. Raise the lettering away from the background by placing several small blocks of paper or rubber eraser on the back of every letter. Use cement to fasten blocks to letters and letters to backgrounds.

Cut out an egg-shaped oval in the proper size. Use this as a foundation shape, drawing the profile and head line within and around it. Make the features bold rather than delicate, so they will cast a strong shadow. There need be no modeling on this flat surface.

The next step is to cut out and apply the various shapes for the eyebrow, the eyelid with lashes, and the lips. In the diagram below are outlined shapes that were used for the heads in the photographs. The slightest change in size or shape will alter the expression or change the character of the head. Each head arrangement you design will be quite different from any other. Tabs on the eyelid were left in order to fasten the shape on both sides to the background head shape. The same is true of the lip shape except that the point at the end slips through to be fastened with scotch tape on the back. The eyelashes may be a part of the eyelid, or separate. They should be long enough to curl. Keep the eyebrows short and arched.

When the features are in place, arrange for the hair. Cut a number of oval and round shapes which are cut into curved strips. Cut from the edge toward a center point, always on a sharp curve. Score each strip on another curved line. Fold back on this line for a sharp edge. You should have more clusters of curled locks than you can use, because it is necessary to make several arrangements before you find a satisfactory one. Place the clusters in position around the face and to cover the back of the head so there seems to be a flowing direction to the hair. Start attaching the hair shapes around the lower edge, letting each new piece cover the place where the first piece is fastened to the head. The final top waves may be cemented in place or folded over the back edge.

Fix the neck, which is a flattened cylinder, to the background before placing the head in position. This will indicate how far away from the back surface, the head need be raised. Cut several strips of paper—wide enough so as not to tear easily. Apply these to the back of the head, with tape in at least three places. Let the ends slip through cuts made previously in the background. Fix in position when the head is in the right spot in relation to the neck.

Collars cover the base of the neck and suggest a width of shoulder. Several suggestions of shapes to be used are shown in the diagram. In most instances a triangular shape can be made to curve around the neck and look like a well-designed collar of a dress. Two more triangles of paper are used for the sleeve and cuff.

The head arrangement shown in the photograph was carried out in colored construction paper. There is a pinkish-tan, flesh-colored paper available which is very satisfactory when used for face, neck and hands. When choosing colors for the rest, keep in mind the effect of strong contrasts in dark and light.

Color can emphasize the sculptural quality but it can also destroy it. Value in color choice is more important than variety.

Punch and Judy

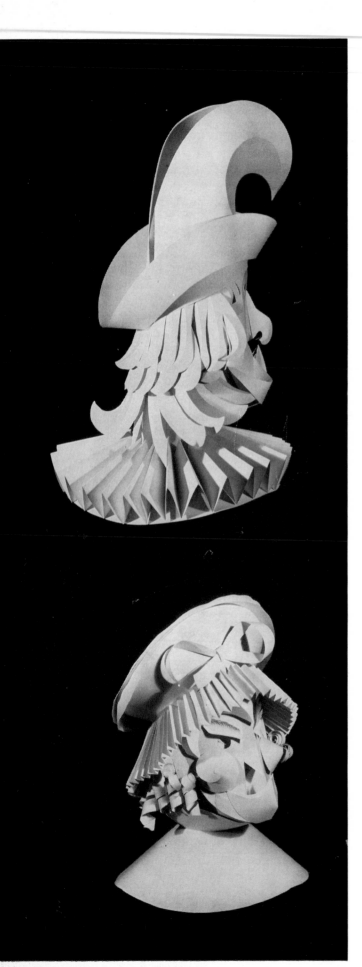

Puppets and puppetry have always had a universal appeal to children. As the prototypes of all puppet characterizations, "Punch and Judy" illustrate what can be done with paper sculpture to produce puppet heads. These models should stimulate the young designer to further attempts at caricature in three dimensions, with scored and folded paper as the medium of design. The heads in the illustration are quite large, big enough to be used in a puppet theater production, but they could be modeled on a smaller scale for hand puppets, or thimble-size for finger puppets. Whether they are to be manipulated in performance or used for purely ornament and decoration, puppet characters are sure to please and interest everyone.

The heads of "Punch and Judy" in the photograph are based on cylindrical forms. The added parts, such as the hooked nose and chin, the rounded cheek, and the lowering brow are built of simple geometric shapes which are in turn fastened to the head cylinder.

The only irregular shape in either design is the one for "Punch's" cap; all others are the whole or part of a geometric shape. A drawing of this odd cap shape is shown below. It is cut from a fold, at an angle to allow the curved tip to curl forward over the face.

Man in the Moon

A child, no matter how inexperienced, who can handle a pair of scissors and make a couple of slashes with a knife point, can be responsible for creating some very interesting caricatures in his "Man in the Moon." For best results the man had better be young in the first quarter or old in the last quarter, for it is the crescent moon that is used.

Make a circular line with a compass, as large as the sheet of paper will accommodate, and with a freehand stroke complete the crescent shape. After this has been cut out, draw the features in profile lightly with pencil along the inside edge. Cut along the penciled line with the scissors. The eye, inside the bridge of the nose, is nothing more than two curved slashes, the mouth is a slightly up-curved cut. A little attention to scoring and folding back around the eye and mouth will produce shadows and make it possible to see clearly the "Man in the Moon."

False Faces for Halloween

False faces for Halloween frolics or thought provoking character masks can be fashioned in paper sculpture with equal ease. The masks can be worn in pantomime or used for decorative purposes.

The two masks illustrated are developed on the basis of an oval shape. Fold a piece of paper through the center vertically and cut both sides of the head shape at one time. If a smooth rounded face without the center crease is desired, use the first cutout as a pattern to draw around. Leave a good-sized tab of paper on either side of the head shape in the position of the ears, to fasten to a band of paper which will pass around the child's head holding the mask in place.

Cut out two spots to see through, another so the tip of the nose will be free, and another opening at the mouth. The features may be developed or accented with folds and cuts or they may be made separately and applied to the face oval. Differently shaped openings for the eyes, nose and mouth will completely change the appearance of the face. Locks of hair, ears and hats can be fastened to the oval shape last of all. Leave extra tabs of paper around the edge of an eyebrow, nose, ear or mouth so that they may be passed through slits in the mask and fastened to the wrong side with bits of Scotch Brand tape.

Clown's Head

Here is a simple design that consists almost entirely of a cylinder of paper. This suggestion is well within the scope and ability of a very young artist. Arrangements like the clown's head in the illustration may be used for party decorations or jack'-o'-lanterns; or if they are made large enough, they may be slipped over the youngster's head for pantomime or play.

With the exception of three round shapes, for the chubby cheeks and bulbous nose and two triangular shapes for ears, it is all of one piece of paper. It is basically a stovepipe cylinder.

Measure down from the top edge to the hairline. Cut this section into narrow strips and either bend forward over the forehead or curl into ringlets. The rufflike collar consists of a scored and folded section of uniform slits, cut across the length of the cylinder. Before bending, score a line along the top and bottom of the cuts on the back of the paper. Exactly in the middle and parallel to the top and bottom edges, score and fold a line on the top side of the paper. Now bend the collar into place.

The ears and cheeks are scored, folded, and curved before they are fastened to the head. When they are ready, poke a corner, or an edge of paper through a slit cut into the cylinder and fasten firmly to the inside with scotch tape.

When everything is in place, ease the flat piece of paper back into the original form of a cylinder and fasten it securely.

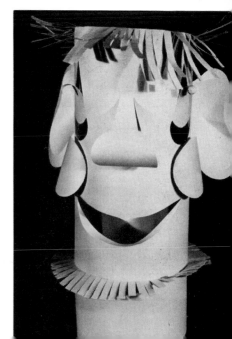

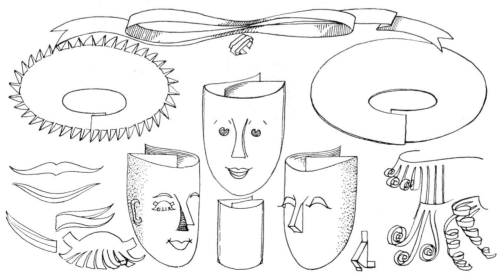

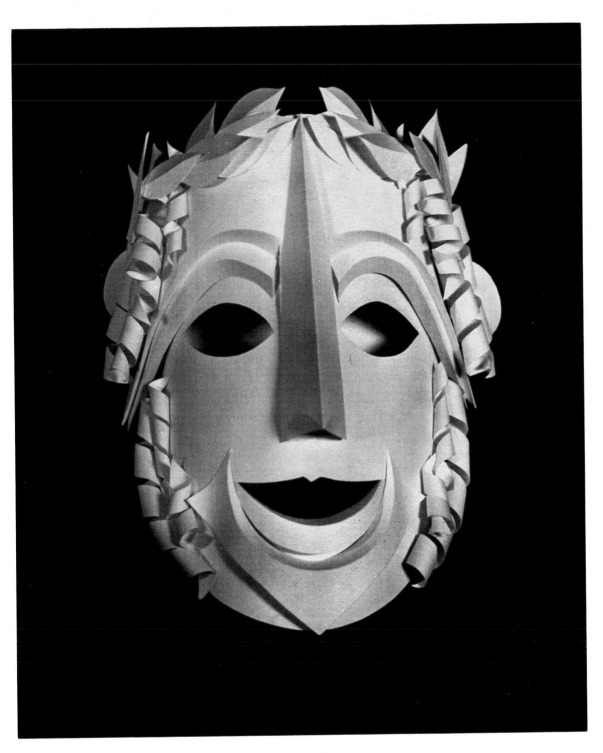

Grecian Mask

Masks of Comedy and Tragedy

PAPER-SCULPTURED MASKS have proved most effective when used for decorative purposes. The symbols of the theater were chosen to illustrate because they may be used in so many different ways in connection with the dramatic activities of the school. Photographed, they make interesting cover designs on programs. Posters advertising dramatic productions may be designed around them. They are striking in mural decorations for lobby and auditorium. Because of exaggeration of shape and line, there are no subtleties to be considered, so it is possible for one of little experience to design a very satisfactory composition.

Start with the face oval. Cut several foundation shapes, similar to the line drawing in the center of the diagram. Make your own design by folding and cutting both sides at once. Each shape may be modified, giving variety to the outline, without changing the size. Cut the face shape slightly wider than the true proportions of the head, for this section must be curved away from the background to show the mask in relief. Note the extra tabs left on either side of the face. These are folded back and finally fastened to a background. While working with the foundation and other parts—keep them flat; do not round them until all pieces are assembled.

Decide where the eyes, nose and mouth are to be placed, and outline them lightly in pencil. Cut out the eyes and mouth with a sharp blade and make a small horizontal slit for the tip of the nose.

Some of the parts shown in the line drawings have extra tabs along some edges. These are left so they may be inserted through slits and fastened with scotch tape on the back of the paper. When slashing through the paper with the tip of the blade, take care that the direction of the cut is the same as the edge of the piece to be applied.

In the upper left-hand and right-hand corners of the diagram are the shapes used for the forehead, brow and nose. The figure for comedy is broad and flat; for tragedy the curves are sharper and the nose is pointed. Score the inner line on the outside and press back to make a deep shadow around the eyes. This piece is arranged so there is space between it and the foundation to create more shadow.

In the lower corners, two shapes are suggested for the cheeks. "Tragedy" must have drooping curves for a downcast expression; "Comedy," round short curves for a gay, happy look. Much depends upon the curved line that is scored and moulded into the shapes desired. These shapes suggesting the muscles of the cheek must be firmly fastened to the first piece by the tab and scotch tape. Wrinkles on the forehead of the tragic mask add to its lowering expression. This is a semicircle, scored in reverse order and attached with tabs.

Use ringlets of hair for the laughing mask and a few tight curls for the tragic one. Short strips, curled, will do for both, but for the lively ringlets, make the fringe long enough to meet at the back. Each strip must be curled separately. Start the curl between two fingers or around a knitting needle. Once it is started it is a simple matter to complete the curl.

The traditional masks are almost always hung from streamers and tied with a bowknot. The ends and lengths of ribbon are uneven strips that are curled at the end and twisted about. Cut a long strip for the bowknot, narrowing it at three equidistant points for each loop. When arranging it into a knotted bow, twist each strip enough to suggest a three-dimensional triangular loop. If you wish to elaborate, use leafy branches secured in the knot.

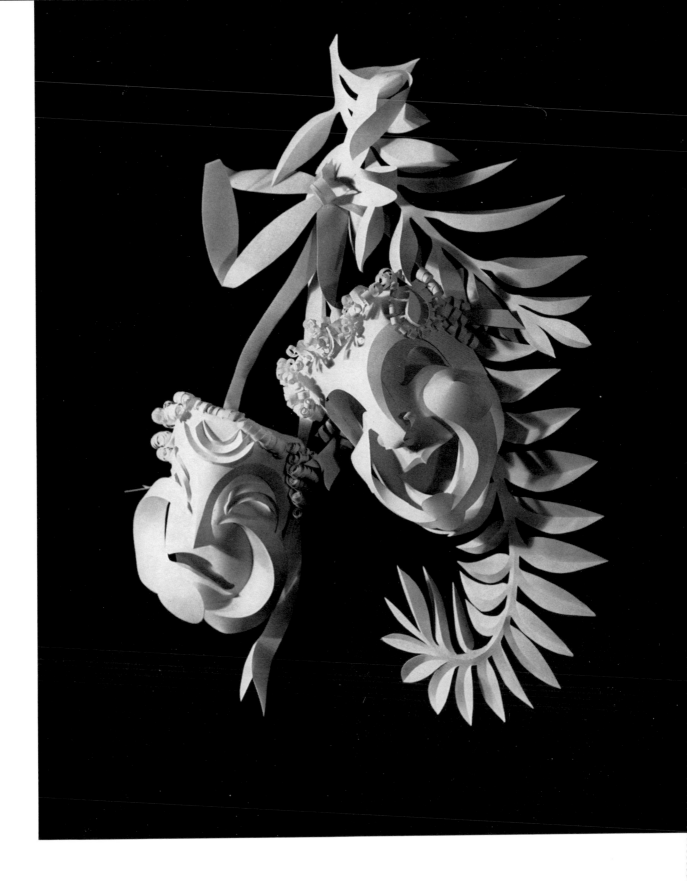

Santa Claus

On this page there is a diagram showing how to fold and cut a five-pointed star. The Santa Claus figure illustrated, with a few folds in the paper, and the addition of a fringe of curled paper for the hair and whiskers, a curved strip of paper for the belt, and five folded round shapes for cuffs and trimmings, is a five-pointed star.

Use triangular pads shown on page 14 fitted into the back angles of the star shape so that the back will present a flat surface to paste against a background. Rubber cement will keep the pads in place without disturbing the surface of the paper. If two-sided masking tape is used, be sure to apply enough pressure to insure the two parts staying together.

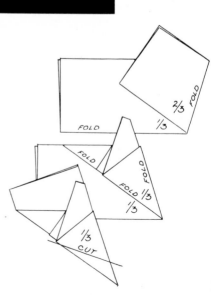

76

Snow Crystals

Holly Wreath

Christmas Angel

Christmas Trees

Few paper sculptured forms give wider latitude in creative expression than these simply constructed Christmas trees. Experimental folding and cutting will bring about new patterns without conscious effort. The youngest and least experienced child can design this type of decoration.

The trees in the illustrations consist of six or eight triangular pieces of paper, folded and cut in such a way as to suggest the form and appearance of a pine tree. The child may choose the size and shape he likes as long as all the triangles are of the same size and shape so that the finished design will be symmetrical.

Before cutting out the triangular shapes, fold each sheet of paper lengthwise through the center with a sharp crease. The shape of the two different triangles used for the two trees in the illustrations, with the suggested cuts and modeling, is shown in the diagram. Cut each section with a center fold, and use the first cutout as a pattern for the other sections.

In the tree design showing the tree trunk, cut from the edge toward the center fold. Cut into strips in a slightly upward direction, leaving enough space at the fold to form the sturdy center tree trunk. Pierce each section along the fold at least three times with a pin or compass point. Be sure these holes occur in identical places on each fold. Run a thread through each point with a needle and tie. Do this with the sections lying flat, then stand them upright and arrange evenly to form a Christmas tree.

The second tree form rests on its lowest branches. Cut from the fold at regular intervals in a downward direction, to a light line that has been measured in from the cut edge on each section. For the tree to look symmetrical the cut strips should go in the same direction and be the same size in each part. This requires measuring before cutting, but if a strip of paper is cut the desired length and width and used to draw around and against, in place of a ruler, measuring becomes a simple matter. The lines in the diagram indicate where each strip of paper has been scored and folded back. Pull the cut

pieces out away from the sides to take the place of branches. Attach one triangular shape to the next along the cut edges, tacking in place lightly with small amounts of *Higgins Vegetable Glue or Sobo.*

Both of the illustrated decorative tree forms were purposely left simple in design. Many variations of the cuts and folds will be suggested as the child works. As both sides of the paper show in these designs, it is worthwhile to sometimes use coated papers and silver and gold foil papers; but the height of the trees should be under twelve inches if lightweight paper is used. Heavy paper will support a design as large as thirty-six inches tall, without a center brace.

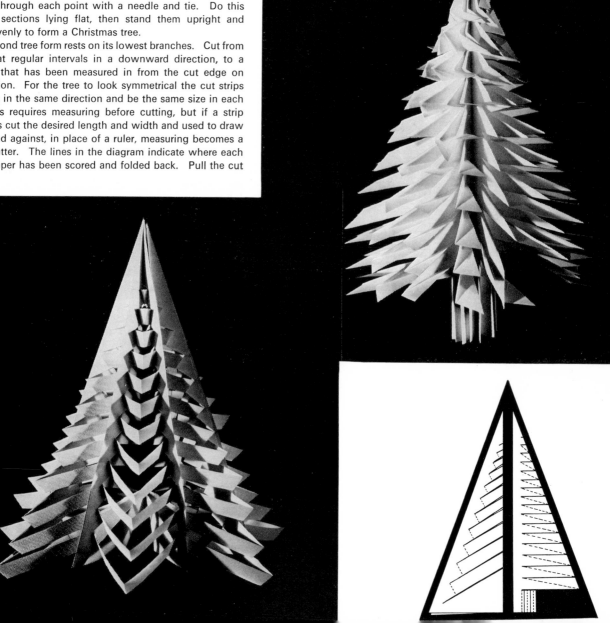

Party Hats

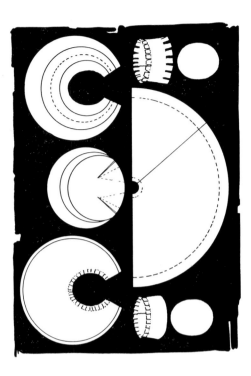

(3) the brimmed cap. There are many variations of each of these classes.

The four hats shown on this page are modeled in heavy white paper. One is a close fitting bonnet to be worn on the back of the head, two are poke bonnets with flaring curved brims to frame the face of the wearer, and the fourth is a tall hat, a jester's hat, which might also be the beginning of any tall crowned hat. All four are cut, scored, and folded from circular pieces of paper. Little trimming has been added so that the construction of each shape shows clearly in the photograph. With the illustration are line analyses of each hat.

The first consideration in designing any hat is to have it fit the head for which it is made. A hat should stay on without being tied on or pinned. Model the brim of a hat, make sure it rests comfortably, then construct the crown and attach it to the brim. Most crowns slope gently in toward the top; therefore, the sides of most crowns will be cut from a wide rim of a circular shape of paper. The top of a crown may be round or oval. If the poke bonnets are to be tied under the chin with ribbons, use paper for the modeled bow, but attach the bow to actual ribbon or tape for strength.

Construction paper in its full range of color is fine for modeling hats. For large and sweeping brims, use two thicknesses of paper. Take care in scoring that the paper does not break, and fasten parts together with staples, or with glue where the stapler cannot reach.

The few hats in the illustration show some first steps. Many other interesting hats can be developed. Young girls especially will find great satisfaction in combining colors and trimming hats.

Fancy headdress modeled in paper has a practical use as well as an historic and aesthetic value. Hats worn by children in school plays and at parties may contribute to a period costume, add to the attractiveness of a child's personality, or provoke mirth, and add to the fun of the occasion. The ability to model of paper a hat that can be used for fancy dress parties, costume plays, and fashion shows is a decided asset. These hats can be historically correct, fanciful, economical, colorful, and in good taste. Museum and library research in the subject of period headgear will be found both satisfying and rewarding. Through the centuries there have been constant changes in size, trimming, and ways of wearing the hat; but any hat falls into one of three basic categories: (1) the skull cap or bonnet, (2) the draped turban, and

For

Valentine's

Day

Crowns for the May Queen

One large sheet of heavy white paper or gold foil covered paper will yield at least three regal crowns for the queen's choice. These symbols of sovereignty, carved out of paper, may resemble crowns of historic interest or they may be the product of the child's imagination. Each of the crowns illustrated is based on a regular, evenly curved strip of paper cut from a whole or a part of a circular shape. It will not be necessary to draw and plan on a complete circular shape. Any wedge shape which measures more than a quarter circle and less than a half circle will be sufficient. Use a common center when making the several arcs that will enclose the curved strip on which the pattern is arranged. The rims cut away furthest from the center point will have the least flare, and will stand almost erect. Those sections cut nearest the center of the circle will spring outward at a more acute angle.

Use a center point for the circular lines on the extreme edge of the long side of the sheet of paper about a quarter of the whole length in from the corner. With a radius equal to the width of the sheet of paper swing as long a circular line as the size of the paper permits. Decide upon the height of the first crown, and that distance inside the first curved line make another. Measure the height of the second crown, reduce the radius by that distance and draw another curved line. Repeat this performance for the third crown. As the decoration around the crown occurs at regular intervals, measurements must be made from the common center through the several arcs to the outside line. Cut the crown shapes apart, only after deciding on all divisions and space relationships, and when the center point for the circular lines is no longer needed. Schoolroom compasses are often too small to use in designing large scale circular forms. Use a length of strong thread or cord tied to the point of a pencil for a radius, and hold the cord to a center point with a thumbnail. Draw the curved line with the pencil held in a vertical position.

The design in the three crowns in the illustration was developed by cutting into radiating sections, scoring, and folding forward or backward edges or pieces of freed paper. Scoring and folding a strip of paper strengthens it so that the crown will stand firmly in an upright position. Try to use all of the paper within the design; fold rather than cut away. Any space division repeated at regular intervals will produce a design that suggests exquisite ornament.

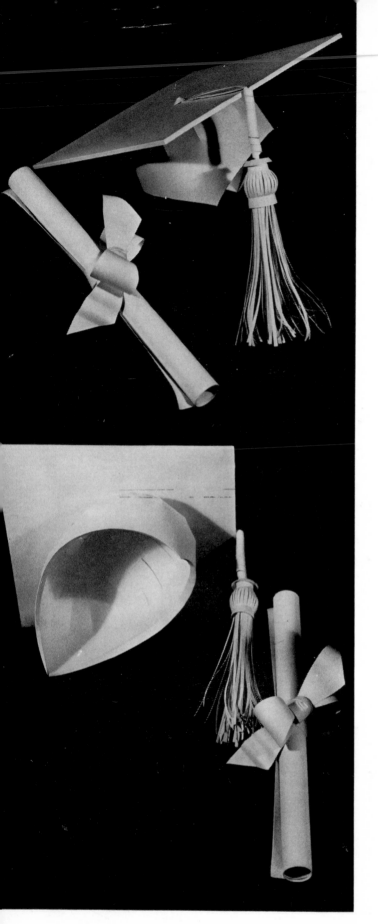

Academic Cap and Diploma

Graduation festivities and exercises often call for decorations, ornaments, and party favors such as the mortar-board and the diploma illustrated here. Students who have enough skill and sense of perspective can design forms in low relief, but designs done in the round are also useful.

In making the academic cap illustrated, the close fitting crown and the flat top are modeled separately and fastened together when complete. The cap can be made full size, to be worn in procession, or small enough to adorn a place card. The diagram below shows the steps taken in cutting, scoring, and folding the paper for the cap. The tassel can be as simple or as elaborate as the student desires. It starts with a length of paper slashed in narrow strips, which are rolled into a hard, knotlike shape at one end. Ornamental bindings may be wrapped around this core. For the cord, a long strip of paper is scored through the center, folded, and cut close to the fold. This cord is doubled again and fastened through the center of the flat mortar-board surface with a button. A short section of the cord hangs over one edge, and the free end is fastened to the tassel.

For the diploma, a rectangular sheet of paper was rolled over a pencil until the thickness of the roll was right for its length. Then it was bound in place with a narrow strip of pressure-sensitive tape. The two corners that show were curled enough to break the smooth surface of the roll.

A long, narrow strip of paper was cut for the bow. Starting from one end of the strip, the shape of one end, a loop, a center, a second loop, and the other end were cut with scissors, in that order, finishing at the other end of the strip. The ends and the loops were curled over with a dull knife blade, and the strip was folded in place so that all the narrow sections coincided. Then the bow was bound together with a strip of paper. The ribbon binding around the middle of the diploma is a separate shape and is scored and folded at each end to look crushed. Sobo, the new quick drying white glue makes an excellent adhesive for small pieces of paper like these.

The cap and the diploma may be hung as mobiles or arranged against a curtain or a wall; or modeled in low relief, they may be used on posters and announcements.

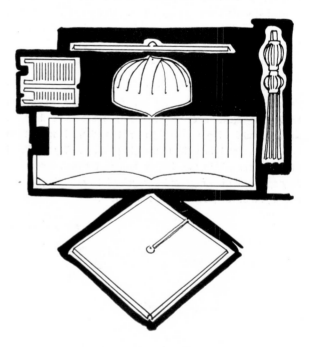